Parenting The Highly Sensitive Child:

*Effective Parenting Strategies
to Unlock the full potential of Your Child's
gift and thrive in an overwhelming world*

ELENA JENKINS

Table of Contents

Introduction

As many parents do, Ann and Mark assumed that taking their young son Carl to the newly opened theme park would be a great surprise for his 4th birthday. Festive colors, fun games, exhilarating rides—what more could a child ask for? Sure, there may be many people there, and coupled with the heat of the summer, it might become a little uncomfortable at some point.

Still, they believed that the pros outweighed the cons. The special birthday plan pushed through.

Carl, unfortunately, did not appreciate the surprise. He stood frozen for a bit as he tried to get a grasp of what was going on, strangers here and there, loud noises seemingly from everywhere. The roller coaster with its screaming passengers frightened him, as well as the gigantic tiger mascot with its flashy jumper.

Ann and Mark thought that Carl only needed a bit of persuasion. After all, some of their treasured memories as kids involved themed parks and carnivals.

Eventually, Carl felt bad about making a fuss, so he gave in. He tried his best to find things that he could enjoy and appreciate. Unfortunately, the heat was getting to him, and his feet were starting to hurt because of his new sneakers.

And so, somewhere in the middle of the themed park, Carl just stopped walking, and tears sprang from his eyes. He couldn't stop it—nobody could. Carl felt awful and helpless, and he couldn't explain why when his parents kept asking what was wrong.

What was supposed to be a fun-filled birthday turned into a stressful incident that neither Carl nor his parents would easily forget.

Has anything similar ever happened to you and your child?

Do you think your child cries or startles more easily than the other kids you know?

Is your child picky when it comes to their food, clothes, hobbies, or even the blanket they use at night?

Can your child quickly notice that something has changed in the way you dress or the way you arrange the house?

If you find yourself nodding to some—if not all—of these questions, then you probably have a highly sensitive child.

Though parenting involves some trial and error, you don't have to be like Ann and Mark, who realized this a little too late.

This book is going to prevent you from unwittingly exposing your highly sensitive child to situations that are distressful and overwhelming for them. It shall also prevent you from misunderstanding what high sensitivity means in the first place and why you should adopt certain parenting strategies that have been proven to work well with highly sensitive children.

Since you have picked my book to serve as your guide, you are already on the right track towards becoming the ideal parent for your highly sensitive child. I'm confident that my years of experience in raising a child gifted with high sensitivity would greatly help you. Like you, I took the time to understand my child better and figure out how to best fulfill his needs and wants. Along the way, I also learned that my goal as a parent isn't to mold my child into what I thought was good or right. And now, through this book, I hope that other parents would also understand and accept this.

How are we going to reach such goals together?

Across different chapters, I will explain carefully to you what high sensitivity truly means. You will also get to know the various ways in how you could help your child cope with different challenges in their day-to-day life—may it be in your home, with their friends, or even at school. By the end of it, you will feel empowered to raise a highly sensitive child and guide them into becoming a healthy, happy, and successful individual.

No more misconceptions or wrong approaches. No more unnecessary tears or traumatic experiences. Read through each chapter of this book, and I will show you how you can be the best parent for your highly sensitive child.

Don't jump to the conclusion that something is wrong with being highly sensitive, though. Yes, it can be challenging for both the children and their parents. It may impose limitations that other kids do not have to live with. However, if you think about it, the same applies to other qualities that are perceived by many as normal, such as being introverted or having a low aptitude for arts and craft projects.

As repeatedly emphasized by numerous child development experts, such as Dr. Elaine Aron and Professor Michael Pluess, high sensitivity is a personality trait that 1 in 5 individuals may have. It is not a mental disorder that requires treatment or medication. It is not something that should be changed or forced out of your child's system.

The numerous parenting tips and strategies shared in this book are backed by these objective research studies, as well as my experience as a parent to a highly sensitive child like yours. Though not everything is guaranteed to work because each highly sensitive child has unique needs and personalities, try to apply the advice and tips shared in this book, and see which ones would work best for your child.

Don't try to overthink this and assume that traditional parenting methods would work on highly sensitive children, too. Going the extra mile for your kid would be worth all your time and effort once you see them growing up to their full potential and making the most of the opportunities they receive along the way.

Through this book, you will be guided at every step of the way. You will no longer find yourself second-guessing if your parenting strategies are beneficial for your highly sensitive child. You likely won't be in a dreadful situation like Ann and Mark, nor will your child have to repeatedly suffer from overwhelming experiences as Carl did.

Thank you for choosing this book! I can't wait to share with you everything I know about raising a highly sensitive child the right way. Remember to take notes as you read, and feel free to share them with me in your review of this book afterward.

Part 1:

Recognizing Traits and Misconceptions

Chapter 1:
Highly Sensitive Child Traits

D oes your child cry or startle easily? Do you think your child expresses happiness or sadness more intensely? Does your child become suddenly shy when facing unfamiliar people or situations?

If you find yourself nodding your head at these questions, then your child may be highly sensitive.

To help you recognize these signs more accurately, this chapter shall tackle the common traits associated with highly sensitive children.

Do You Have a Highly Sensitive Child?

Derived from the intensive research work of Dr. Elaine Aron, the checklist below can be used to determine if your child possesses traits that are associated with high sensitivity. Go over each item on the checklist, and count the number of qualities that you believe are exhibited by your child. Remember to count only the items that are either true or moderately true about your child, and leave out the items that do seem to be true or only somewhat true.

- Seems to be able to predict or read the mind of others
- Has a witty or clever sense of humor
- Exhibits a high level of intuition
- Has a hard time accepting or adjusting to big changes
- Reflects deeply about his/her experiences
- Has deep, intense feelings of joy, sadness, anger, and fear
- Sensitive to feelings of distress felt by others
- Easy to cry or throw a tantrum
- Can get upset over small things
- Easy to startle
- Sensitive to even the slightest change in odor
- Responds better to gentle guidance rather than strong reprimands
- Feels restless after experiencing an exciting or active day
- Cannot stand wet or sandy clothes at all
- Cannot stand noisy places
- Picky about food and drinks
- Quick to notice subtle changes in the position or appearance of people or things around him/her

- Likes using words that seem to be too big for his/her age
- Asks plenty of questions, including hard or thoughtful ones
- Perfectionist
- Prefers playing alone or in a quiet environment
- Hesitates when asked to climb something high
- Slow to warm up to new people

If 13 or more of the above-given qualities are exhibited by your child, then you likely have a highly sensitive child. Moreover, even if only one or two qualities apply to your child, he/she might also be highly sensitive if you believe that those qualities are extremely true.

How did your child score according to this checklist? Do not hesitate or be afraid if the score points to the likelihood that you have a highly sensitive child. As you will learn later on in this book, high sensitivity is not a problem but rather an opportunity for you to guide your child into growing up as a healthy and accomplished individual.

In case that you are not sure how to recognize the traits are given above, the next section shall discuss these in greater detail.

Understanding the Traits of a Highly Sensitive Child

There is no universal combination of traits that make up the personality and behavior of a highly sensitive child. Instead, the child would likely exhibit a few of these traits consistently. The traits would also be quite evident because their manifestation tends to be in a more extreme form than what you may be used to. These reactions, attitudes, and behavioral patterns are also a product of their perception of their surroundings and the people around them.

Though the list below is not exhaustive, the following traits are the more commonly observed ones by child psychologists, teachers, parents, and caretakers of highly sensitive children:

- Pays a lot of attention to their surroundings

  Highly sensitive children have keen senses and sharp intuition, both of which enhance their observational skills. These kids pay attention to the characteristics, behavior, and habits of the people around them. Using this information, they try to form an idea about the personalities of others, and more often than not, they can come up with accurate

19

readings.

Aside from people, children with high sensitivity are also observant of their immediate environment. They notice right away the colors, smells, and texture of the things around them. They can also be quite affected by the temperature and humidity of the area, which could cause them to feel either irritated or upset.

Because of their excellent observational skills, highly sensitive kids are quick to discern changes in people, such as mood, feelings, appearance, or physical condition. It is almost like it is part of their nature to assess the person's current condition or environment before them. They would then compare this assessment to their previous knowledge and pinpoint the differences if there are any.

- Asks a lot of questions

  Most children are naturally curious about almost anything and everything under the sun. Highly sensitive children take this quality up a notch. They tend to ask one question after another—sometimes to the point of irritating the other party.

Their questions can also border on personal ones that might make others uncomfortable. However, their intention is not to breach the privacy of the people around them but rather to satisfy their curiosity and ultimately learn more about the subject matter at hand.

- Takes a long time to decide

Studies indicate that highly sensitive children make deliberate but firm decisions. They take their time in looking and assessing the details of the situation, even the subtle points that normally escape the attention of less sensitive people. This particular trait manifests regardless of how big or small the decision is. It could be as simple as choosing a flavor of juice to drink, or picking a game to play.

Because of the amount of time and effort that they give when it comes to making a decision, highly sensitive children stand by their choice as much as they can. Their emotions are also at play, so if the decision ends up becoming a mistake, they feel the outcome deeply and personally. The great thing is, they admit their mistakes, and even though it can be detrimental when taken to an extreme, they also feel accountable for the consequences that their mistake has caused.

- Becomes greatly affected by failures

  Much like wrong decisions, failures make a big impact on a highly sensitive child's wellbeing. When such kids fail to achieve their target, they will spend a lot of time thinking about the things that led to a poor outcome. Usually, this line of thinking would lead to brooding about why they did not recognize the bad turning point in time.

  If not guided properly, this trait may cause highly sensitive children to suffer from elevated stress levels and anxiety. On the other hand, if taught how to handle failures constructively and healthily, these kids can think of failures as opportunities to learn about how to do better next time, and how to keep themselves from making the same mistakes again in the future.

- Reacts in an emotional manner

  Almost anything could elicit an emotional reaction from highly sensitive children. Whether it is a positive or negative experience, their feelings will be moved to a great extent. Experts say this is caused by their naturally high level of empathy.

For example, a reprimand from a teacher may reduce the child into tears. Seeing others in pain could also make them feel worried and distressed about what they can do to turn around the situation. Conversely, a happy moment with friends or pets would be quite delightful and memorable for them, too.

Due to their highly emotional nature, these kids also take words and actions by others personally. Regardless of the actual intention, they tend to believe that the words or actions are aimed only at them. Therefore, praises and positive comments have an even greater boosting effect on them, while scolding and bad remarks may be devastating for them.

- Forms a special bond with animals

  Studies show that highly sensitive children tend to be extra attentive to the needs of animals. Because of this, these kids know how to better take care of them. Over time, mutual trust will be developed between the children and animals. A bond that is based on mutual trust forms the foundation of their special bond.

As you may have noticed, the traits of highly sensitive children are not limited only to sensitivity to stimuli but also to their mental capabilities and behavioral patterns. They react intensely to most situations because they process their experiences more deeply. Unlike some people's assumptions, these kids are not focused only on themselves and what they feel—they also show care and empathy towards people, animals, and surroundings.

Take note that none of these traits are absolutely and permanently negative. With proper care and guidance, some of the less helpful ones can be turned into something constructive or at least not as detrimental as they should have been. This is quite important to keep in mind since your goal as a parent is not to force a change to happen but rather to accept and understand the needs and preferences of your child as a highly sensitive person.

Chapter 2:
Different Types of Highly Sensitive Children
(Orchid, Tulip, and Dandelion)

What does it mean if your highly sensitive child is categorized as an orchid, tulip, or dandelion? How were these categories developed? Do they matter in your goal of becoming a better and more nurturing parent for your highly sensitive child?

In this chapter, you will learn about the origins and meaning of the three main categories of highly sensitive children, as well as how each could affect your parenting strategy.

The Environmental Sensitivity Scale for Children

Over the years, there have been many debates about the influence of the environment on the development of children. Several experts nowadays agree that various environmental factors and life experiences affect a child's growth. However, the extent of their influence remains a question that gives rise to further studies.

One theory posits that some children are more affected than others because of their high sensitivity to the environment. To help test this out, a group of UK-based researchers led by Professor Michael Pluess conducted a study among over 300 children and developed a 12-item scale for Environmental Sensitivity.

Ranging from ages 11 to 14, these children were assessed using an existing scale that measures the environmental sensitivity of adults. From the results of this study, Pluess and his team arrived at the 12 items they had observed to be applicable for children.

Going over the contents of the 12-item scale, you will notice that each item could fall under the three primary factors related to environment sensitivity: sensory threshold, degree of excitation, and aesthetic preferences.

From the data they have gathered, the research team has reached the following conclusions:

- The majority of the children tested exhibited less sensitivity to either positive or negative environmental factors. They are categorized as the "dandelions" because the flower is known for being able to withstand and even thrive even if their environment does not have the ideal conditions for growing plants.

- On the other hand, only a small fraction of participating children had shown signs that they are environmentally sensitive. Categorized as "orchids", these children are likened to the delicate nature of the said flower. For orchids to flourish, the caretaker must ensure that its environment is suitable and well-protected from harsh elements.

More recent data, however, suggest an entirely different picture. Instead, they indicate that both the "dandelions" and "orchids" each contribute to around 30% of the data set, while the remaining fall under the "tulip" category, wherein the environmental sensitivity of the children is somewhere between the two other categories.

Regardless of the actual distribution among the three categories, the more important takeaway point from their study is that children's environmental sensitivity can be measured objectively. When something can be measured, you may use it as a foundation for strategies and action plans on how to better nurture your child. You are aware of how sensitive they are to what is around them, and that could serve as a starting point on how you could create an environment where they could grow and thrive.

Nature vs. Nurture

Are "orchids", "tulips", and "dandelions" born this way, or are they a product of how they were brought up?

Various research studies show that it may be a combination of both factors. Certain genes have been associated with high sensitivity. However, possessing that gene does not automatically mean that the individual would exhibit this trait. Instead, they are genetically predisposed to being more sensitive than average.

Some individuals also have high sensitivity even without having these genes. Researchers suggest that this trait may also be developed based on the early childhood experiences of the person. Again, this does not mean that those who have been subjected to abuse or neglect would automatically become either "orchids" or "dandelions". Several child development experts agree that nature and nurture both play a role in the degree of sensitivity that a person would have.

Important Takeaway Points

Though the 12-item environmental sensitivity scale developed by Pluess does not pinpoint the exact environmental sensitivity of the children, it provides an insight on how parents—and even teachers—could better understand and attend to the needs and preferences of highly sensitive children to nurture them into becoming healthy and well-adjusted individuals.

How so?

First, the study conducted by the researchers is under the premise that none of these categories is better than the others. Each type denotes certain qualities that could be considered as either strength or weakness. More importantly, the researchers believe that sensitivity is inherently not a problem to be solved. Instead, it is a strength that can be honed into becoming a tool for achieving greater heights.

For example, in one study, teenage girls who are identified as "orchids" have exhibited greater responsiveness towards therapy efforts to combat depression compared to "dandelions" and "tulips". In another study, "orchids" tend to benefit more from the positive experiences in their lives compared to the other groups. However, this also makes them more vulnerable to the harmful effects of negative experiences, especially those that result from pain and trauma.

This runs contrary to initial conclusions made by researchers, wherein highly sensitive children get significantly affected only by negative factors in their environment. Rather than viewing these children as being at a disadvantage, think of their increased sensitivity as an opportunity for both you and them. "Orchids" and certain "Tulips" have the chance to be exceptional if they have grown in an ideal and positive environment. On the other hand, "Dandelions" and other "Tulips" would flourish if given the resources to explore new experiences and unfamiliar situations since they tend to be resilient and open to changes in their environment.

Recognizing the idea that different children may have different reactions to the same stimuli or experiences is a necessary step towards a parenting style and strategies that can help highly sensitive children thrive even when they are faced with rather challenging situations. Consider asking your child to take the Environmental Sensitivity Scale to assess their actual disposition. Remember to explain to them the importance of doing so and allow them to see it as a self-discovery experience that could guide them into gaining a better understanding of themselves.

Chapter 3:
Is Highly-Sensitive Person (HSP) a Mental Disorder?

The short, simple answer is no.

HSP is not a mental disorder but rather a part of one's personality that is neither inherently good nor bad. Research indicates that high sensitivity can be a beneficial quality when the person has been nurtured and guided well, especially during the formative years.

To better understand HSP, let's go over how the theory behind it was first introduced, how it affects one's daily life, and how it compares to other similar personality traits and actual mental disorders.

Research-Based Theories about HSP

As one of the leading researchers in this field, Dr. Elaine Aron first coined the term "Highly Sensitive Person". She explained that individuals who possess this trait have an elevated capacity for sensory processing sensitivity (SPS). As a result, they react strongly and emotionally to various forms of stimuli from their surroundings, such as noise, heat, light, odors, and smells. Furthermore, their mental processes take a more deliberate and profound route, which results in more insightful observations and understanding of people and the realities of the world.

The important thing to note about Dr. Aron's research is that she did not classify HSP as a mental disorder. Based on her observations, everyone possesses the sensitivity trait but to different degrees. HSP just so happened to be on the end of the scale where they get affected more by various stimuli and experiences.

If you would recall from the previous chapter, this is in line with the study conducted by Dr. Pluess and his team, wherein he posited that children fall into any of the three categories of environmental sensitivity—ranging from the hardy "dandelions", the flexible "tulips", and the delicate "orchids". Moreover, HSP follows the theory that the trait manifests according to the genetic makeup and early childhood experiences of the individual.

Some people assume that this trait is unusual or even rare. However, highly sensitive persons comprise around 15% to 20% of the total population, according to Dr. Aron. With the popularization of the theory over the years, more and more people have also identified themselves as HSP. As a result, several researchers continue to study the theory to better understand how highly sensitive people could be nurtured into becoming healthy and thriving individuals.

Living as a Highly Sensitive Person

Though high sensitivity can be an adaptive advantage in certain scenarios, it can also be a burden, especially when the person has not received proper guidance and sound advice from their parents, teachers, or therapists. In such cases, they may struggle to control their emotions, manage their reactions to other people and their environment, and accept the changes in their lives.

For instance, HSPs quickly leave or avoid overwhelming situations. They cannot stand conflict and tension because their impact is much greater than those with lesser sensory processing sensitivity. This becomes more pronounced if the situation involves their family, friends, or loved ones because HSPs tend to form deeper bonds with the people they care about. They take words and actions seriously and personally, so the hurt caused by their emotions and ego tends to be magnified to a much greater degree.

Other pitfalls that could be quite challenging to overcome for HSPs include the following:

- Not reaching their goals
- Not meeting the expectations of others
- Juggling a hectic schedule
- Facing a high-pressure situation
- Being in an environment that is excessively noisy, smelly, or disorganized

Fortunately, various coping methods have been developed by experts for HSP. While adults can learn them through therapy, these measures can also be taught early on by parents or teachers to children with high sensitivity. Doing so would give a chance for the child to develop their ways of adapting to their environment and situations.

Living with high sensitivity comes with a lot of positives, too. Such individuals perceive and appreciate the beauty in the people around them as well as their surroundings. They also feel moved by heart-warming and touching subject—for example, watching an episode of their favorite TV drama or listening to a beautiful song. Because of this, HSPs are known for expressing gratitude for the good things they have in life. They understand that not everything around them is positive and beneficial for them, but that will not stop them from acknowledging moments in their life that made them feel things on another level.

Understanding the Difference between HSP and Other Traits

Some of the characteristics associated with HSP seem to be similar to those of other traits, such as introversion and neuroticism. However, according to Dr. Aron's research, HSP cannot be viewed as synonymous with such traits because a person may possess HSP and those personality traits. For example, around 70% of highly sensitive individuals also consider themselves introverts, while the remainder identifies themselves as extroverts.

Given this, a person's threshold for excitement, social interactions, and other related factors to the introversion-extraversion spectrum is not entirely determined by their level of sensitivity. Yes, introverts and HSPs may both feel overwhelmed when faced with situations that go beyond their limits. However, introverts tend to feel this way because they generally prefer to be alone, while HSPs feel over-sensitized by the sensations or emotions at play.

On the other hand, extroverts can also be highly sensitive even though they enjoy engaging in stimulating and social activities. Unlike extroverts who do not possess this trait, extroverted HSPs may still be described by others as shy since they tend to take their time to warm up to a new or unfamiliar person and situation.

Some people also equate HSPs with empaths. The latter are described as individuals who can easily read and understand the moods of the people around them. While this may sound like an HSP's good observational skills and insightful reflections about people, the abilities of empaths are believed to be psychic—something that is not included in Dr. Aron's original theory about a highly sensitive person.

HSP and Mental Health

As mentioned earlier, HSP is not a mental disorder. However, because of its nature, experts have noted that some people who possess this trait experience unique and more intense challenges, especially in managing their emotions and relationships with other people. Research also shows that high sensitivity could lead to depression and anxiety, especially if the person does not practice self-care measures like having a balanced diet, lessening alcohol intake, or sleeping for the right amount of time.

Since HSP is not a mental disorder, no treatment could be done to "remove" it or mitigate its effects. Still, mental health experts recommend therapy so that they can better cope with the stress and worries brought about by their high level of sensitivity.

Some people also assume that HSP is the same as a mental health condition known as Sensory Processing Disorder (SPD). Though a highly sensitive person exhibit increased sensory processing sensitivity, Dr. Aron and her team argue that the few similarities that exist between the two do not mean that they are the same. The next chapter will discuss this further to help you differentiate and better recognize the signs of HSP from the symptoms of SPD.

Moreover, HSP has also been observed among individuals with either autism or Attention Deficit Hyperactivity Disorder (ADHD). Though high sensitivity is considered as one of the symptoms of these disorders, HSP remains to be a personality trait in such cases. To help you better understand why experts insist on keeping the distinction between HSP and these mental disorders, the following few chapters will also cover the relationship of HSP with autism and ADHD.

Chapter 4:

The Difference Between Sensory Processing Sensitivity (SPS) and Having Sensory Processing Disorder

Some people confuse sensory processing sensitivity (SPS) with sensory processing disorder (SPD). As such, they automatically assume that being highly sensitive is a symptom of a mental disorder.

However, as you have learned in the previous chapter of this book, SPS is a characteristic that serves as the foundation of a highly sensitive person. It is a part of one's personality, not an abnormality that should be treated. Though HSPs tend to face challenges because of it, this trait can also be a strength when honed properly.

On the other hand, SPD is a neurological condition that creates trouble in one's day-to-day life. It has diagnosable symptoms as well as treatments, much like other mental health problems.

To better understand the difference between the two, this chapter shall discuss the differences between SPS and SPD in greater depth.

Sensory Processing in a Nutshell

The human body and mind receive information from the world around them through the five primary sensory systems: visual (seeing), auditory (hearing), olfactory (smelling), gustatory (tasting), and tactile (touching). Over the years, experts have also noted that sensory information can also be felt from within. This observation gave rise to the three additional sensory systems, which are vestibular (movements of the head through space), proprioceptive (movements of body muscle and joint), and interoception (sensations from internal organs).

Each person has the natural ability to process sensory information. This happens with little to no conscious effort or deliberate thought, except when you are trying to heighten your senses or if you are looking for a specific sensation.

The various sensory systems contribute to the kind of person that you will become. They can influence how you view yourself, your preferences in different aspects of life, as well as how you interact with other people and your surroundings.

Even during infancy, sensory processing is necessary for the baby to discover the world around them and develop various cognitive and motor skills. It is also responsible for building up one's tolerance levels and resilience. By experiencing and processing different stimuli in various situations, you would develop your way of handling stressful situations, overcoming tough challenges, and recovering from failures.

Given how influential your sensory systems are in the development of your body and mind, any deviations in the normal processing of sensory information may have a significant impact on one's physical wellness and mental health.

Sensory Processing Sensitivity and HSP

As mentioned earlier, SPS is a normal trait that has its benefits and drawbacks. Simply speaking, it only denotes that people possessing SPS have high sensitivity towards stimuli from their environment and from within themselves. If you would recall, this is the core quality of a highly sensitive person (HSP).

SPS is not a special or rare trait, but it can be harnessed in ways that would enable you to exhibit exceptional skills and achieve a higher level of accomplishments. For example, since highly sensitive persons can notice things that escape the attention of others, they may be able to form a deeper understanding of people and their environment. This enables them to form stronger bonds with other people and be strategic in the way they handle things—both of which are considered as the makings of a transformational and visionary leader.

As for its disadvantages, the heightened sensitivity brought about by this trait lowers a person's tolerance for stimulations and capacity for information processing. HSPs are known for not being to withstand situations where too many things are happening at once. They become overwhelmed by the stress and pressure, sometimes to the point where they "shut down" to recover.

Despite such drawbacks, SPS is still not considered a mental disorder. The concurrence of anxiety, depression, and other mental disorders among those who also possess this trait does not mean that everyone with SPS will also suffer from the same problems. Instead, having SPS means that the person would view and experience the world in a different way.

What is Sensory Processing Disorder?

SPD is characterized by inappropriate brain responses

due to a "mix-up" of signals received from the different sensory systems to the brain. It used to be part of the autism spectrum, but recent studies show that it is a distinct mental disorder.

According to recent data, one in twenty individuals has SPD. It may be detected during childhood through clinical evaluations and surveys administered to parents. Higher prevalence has been noted among children with autism and ADHD, which leads to some cases of misidentification because of certain signs and symptoms.

The manifestation of SPD differs from one person to another. For example, one child has been observed to be over-sensitive when it comes to textures that he finds unpleasant. However, he barely reacts when hearing loud noises or bright lights. Another child exhibits a slow reaction towards pain but shows heightened sensitivity towards temperature changes. Children who have poor motor skills and those who seem to have extreme cravings for stimulation may also suffer from SPD.

Researchers have not yet identified the exact cause of this mental disorder. Initial studies indicate that it may be present upon birth, either due to the baby's genetic makeup or certain complications during childbirth. Some data also show that environmental factors may also contribute to the development of SPD.

Treatment for SPD involves the expertise of occupational therapists. Children, in particular, have been noted to be responsive to this. Therapists aim to guide them in organizing the sensory information and integrating various stimuli appropriately into their experiences.

SPS vs. SPD

Aside from their similar-sounding names, over-responsivity is another point of confusion between the two. Highly sensitive people and those with SPD show extreme reactions when faced with stimuli that go beyond their threshold levels.

However, in the case of HSPs, their daily lives are not extremely hampered by the way they process sensory information. They can even learn methods on how to reduce the impact or how to respond correctly to situations that may cause them to become overstimulated. People with SPD cannot do this without undergoing therapy that is specifically designed to treat this disorder.

Moreover, HSPs do not normally have under-responsivity towards certain types of stimuli. They process sensory information deeply and deliberately, but signals from sensory systems do not get lost along the way.

To help parents, teachers, and therapists better differentiate HSP from SPD, Dr. Aron developed a questionnaire that aims to examine the different facets of a child's sensory processing, which are:

- Depth of Processing
  This section deals with how the child reflects on their experiences, makes decisions, and comes up with ideas that they put into action. HSP children are known for their insightful thoughts, deliberate choices, and good ideas. On the other hand, children with SPD do not necessarily exhibit these qualities unless they also possess the SPS trait.

- Overstimulation
  Though both highly sensitive children and those with SPD become overstimulated easily, the natures of this extreme response are different. HSPs experience overstimulation due to the volume of stimuli in their surroundings,

while children suffering from SPD are over-stimulated when signals from their sensory system do not get delivered correctly to the right areas of the brain.

- Emotional Responsiveness and Empathy
  HSP feels things deeply and expresses intense emotions. They also relate easily to other people and even animals, especially when they have enough time to get a good reading of them. On the other hand, children with SPD are not consistently observed to be either emotionally responsive or empathetic to others.

- Sensitive to Subtleties
  Children with high sensitive notice subtle details in the people around them and their surroundings. As such, they are quick to identify changes, even small ones that are not easily recognizable. Having SPD does not lead to the development of this high degree of observational skills, however.

This questionnaire may also be used to distinguish HSP from other mental disorders such as autism and ADHD. You will learn more about these differences in the succeeding chapters.

Chapter 5:
The Difference Between High Sensitivity and Autism

By now, you have likely understood why high sensitivity is not considered a mental disorder. However, you might be wondering why some people assume that it is similar to or the same as autism. After all, not so long ago, even experts believe that HSP or sensory processing sensitivity is part of the autism spectrum. They believed that highly sensitive people have mild forms of autism, wherein they could function on a higher level than those who have other types of autism.

Recent studies indicate that this kind of thinking ignores the original theory behind HSP. Moreover, mislabeling it as autism can lead to a poor parenting style and strategies because the needs and preferences of a highly sensitive child differ from one that belongs to the autism spectrum. Therefore, parents and educators need to learn how to differentiate the two.

What are the links connecting high sensitivity to autism? How do they differ? Can a child be highly sensitive and autistic at the same time?

This chapter aims to answer these questions and explain how each could affect a child's growth and development.

Why People Confuse High Sensitivity with Autism

Though high sensitivity and autism are distinct from one another, there are two aspects where they overlap: hypersensitivity and overstimulation.

- Extreme sensitivity levels towards external stimuli

  Both highly sensitive children and autistic children prefer environments and objects that are not too stimulating or unfamiliar. For example, they enjoy playing in a relative place with their favorite toys and playmates who they have already known for a while.

  Moreover, they also feel small or subtle stimulations to a greater degree than most people do. For example, while you would likely not be bothered by the feeling of sand between your toes, they are going to feel the sand grains rubbing against their skin to the point of being irritated by the sensation.

- Tendency to be easily overwhelmed when faced with too many stimuli
Once their thresholds for environmental stimuli have been exceeded, there is a high chance that children with the HSP trait or autism will respond negatively. Common responses to overstimulation include tantrums, sudden feelings of panic, and closing themselves off from their surroundings or other people.

Despite these similarities, HSP remains to be a trait that can be developed into a strength. While autism is gradually being seen in a more positive light recently, it is still officially considered a developmental disorder.

HSP vs. Autism

A 2018 study by a team of neuroscientists from the Neuroscience Research Institute in California examines various research papers about the similarities and differences between high sensitivity and different mental disorders, including autism spectrum disorder (ASD). Through this, they were able to highlight the three primary differences between high sensitivity and autism.

a. Social Deficits

Certain regions of the brain are responsible for processing social and emotional cues. In the case of autistic individuals, lesser brain response has been noted in these parts, thus causing them to exhibit the so-called "social deficits" or behavioral tendencies that are not aligned with how neuro-typical individuals respond to social situations. Among babies, these can be observed as early as two months after their birth.

A common example of a social deficit is making eye contact. Autistic children find it hard to initiate and maintain eye contact. They also do not easily reciprocate a smile, even when it is from someone they already know.

In comparison, highly sensitive people have demonstrated enhanced responsiveness towards social cues. They can recognize the intention of others and respond accordingly to the facial expressions of the person they are interacting with. Neurological findings show that this is caused by the increased activity in the same parts of the brain where autistic individuals indicate lesser responsiveness.

b. Perception of Social Interactions

By nature, human beings find social interactions to be good opportunities to forge strong bonds with the people around them. The ability to communicate and cooperate with others has been key components towards our continued survival.

Autistic individuals, however, do not usually think of social interactions as important, meaningful, and rewarding. Yes, they can form deep relationships, but the act of engaging with other people is not something that they need or crave for. Because of this, they also find it difficult to make appropriate social responses.

In comparison, highly sensitive people demonstrate strong reactions to social interactions. Positive ones make them feel that the interaction is extra rewarding and meaningful for them. Depending on the context, it can make them feel calm, interested, or delighted. Conversely, negative social interactions could knock them off their feet, especially if it is between someone they care about.

c. Response towards Stimuli

Though the same areas of the brain are more active among HSP and autistic individuals when it comes to physical and mental response to stimuli, the actual brain activities that occur in other areas are not the same.

Highly sensitive persons have more brain activity in the parts that are related to deep thinking, calmness, control, and balance of the hormones. Combined with their empathy and sensory processing sensitivity, their response to stimuli tends to be positive in most situations.

People on the autism spectrum, however, have been observed to exhibit lesser brain activity in the said areas. This affects their ability to remain calm, control their emotions, and be sociable in their day-to-day life.

While these differences could be helpful in understanding HSP and autism, remember to seek the professional evaluation of a child development expert rather than making judgment by yourself. Again, this would have a significant impact on how you would guide and nurture your child.

Being on the Autism Spectrum as a Highly Sensitive Person

One's personality traits are distinct from any type of developmental or mental challenge. If you would recall, the previous chapter of this book touches on the fact that a highly sensitive person is at risk of developing anxiety or depression if one's childhood experiences are negative or traumatic. ADHD is another disorder that can be concurrent with high sensitivity, as you would learn in the succeeding chapter. Given these, a child can be highly sensitive and be on the autism spectrum at the same time.

How is this possible when some qualities of a highly sensitive person are vastly different from those of an autistic individual?

The thing is, not all qualities have to be exhibited by the person to be identified as HSP or autistic—as long as the core characteristics are present. As discussed in earlier chapters, high sensitivity is defined by their in-depth processing of sensory information, while repetitive behaviors and verbal and non-verbal communication challenges define those with an autism spectrum disorder.

If this is the case for your child, then you would have

to take into account both conditions in your parenting strategies. Otherwise, you might end up forcing your child into situations that would be damaging to their psyche and overall wellbeing. Again, it is best to refer to professionals before moving forward with your plan for the healthy development of your child.

Chapter 6:
Do Highly Sensitive Children Have ADHD?

High sensitivity does not have many overlapping points with Attention Deficit Hyperactivity Disorder (ADHD), but there are cases wherein highly sensitive children have been diagnosed with this brain condition. Because of this, chances of misidentifying one for another also exist.

How can you tell one from the other? What are the signs that your child possesses the high sensitivity trait while also having ADHD?

Find out the answers to these questions and more in the following sections.

What is ADHD?

ADHD refers to a medical condition wherein certain parts and activities of an affected person's brain are different in ways that affect their ability to pay attention, keep still, and control themselves. You may be able to tell if a child has ADHD if they exhibit at least one of the following signs:

- Inattentiveness

  These children find it hard to concentrate on what they are thinking or doing at the moment. They are also easy to get distracted by the things that are going on around them. As a result, they do not finish a lot of tasks that they were assigned to them.

  When you talk to these children, they might not seem like they are paying attention to what you are saying. You might also notice that they tend to fail to remember the important details. Aside from these, they tend to lose track of their belongings as well, despite being reminded of where they have put them beforehand.

- Hyperactivity

  This may manifest in the form of fidgety movements and general restlessness. If they are told to keep quiet or sit down, they will likely disobey you since they cannot seem to keep themselves from talking or moving around.

  You may see them going around the room, jumping here and there, and sometimes even climbing things that should not be climbed.

More often than not, these behaviors can be disruptive to the people nearby.

Children with ADHD rush through their tasks and activities as well. Because of this, they tend to commit mistakes that could easily have been avoided.

- Impulsiveness

    Acting before thinking gets these children in trouble. They simply cannot wait for their turn or for others to finish speaking. If they feel like they need something, they do not hesitate to grab it and keep it for themselves.

    Their emotions also contribute to their impulsions. They feel things intensely, so if they believe that taking or doing something would make them feel better, they are likely to go ahead and act on their assumptions.

In some cases, parents and teachers can recognize the signs even when the child is young. However, seeking a professional diagnosis from a neurological expert is highly recommended regardless of how sure you are of your observations. After all, young children without ADHD may still be distracted, restless, or impatient, depending on what they are feeling or doing at the moment. What distinguishes ADHD from these misbehaviors is that this persistent and developing condition could cause the child to struggle when it comes to interacting with their family, friends, and other people and performing well at school.

Fortunately, ADHD is treatable. Options that parents may consider include the following:

a. Medication

    These may help in regulating brain activities that are related to the children's attention span, motor activity, and ability to control themselves.

b. Behavioral Therapy

    Through therapy, experts can help children develop the abilities that they lack due to their condition, such as emotional control, capacity to plan, and social skills.

c. Parental Coaching

    Parents also need to learn the right way to respond to the needs of their children with ADHD, especially the ones that arise due to the challenges that they are facing daily.

Educators who are trained on how to properly deal with children that have ADHD can also be a source of support for parents and the kids themselves. They can ensure that the said children would still do well at school in terms of academic performance and social interactions with other students. As a result, children with ADHD may still have a positive school life despite their condition.

Untangling the Confusion Between High Sensitivity and ADHD

Much like with autism, the main overlapping point between high sensitivity and ADHD is overstimulation. In the case of kids with ADHD, parents and teachers tend to notice it when the said children always feel overwhelmed in a crowded or busy area. In schools, these are the kids that start misbehaving or acting differently than usual in group activities. At home, children with ADHD cannot cope with spending too much time with multiple siblings or playmates. As discussed in previous chapters of the book, highly sensitive children are not able to stand in similar environments or situations as well.

However, the similarities between the two end there. When children with the high sensitivity trait get overstimulated, their usual responses include panicking, "shutting down" themselves or throwing a tantrum. In comparison, children with ADHD could have either of the two responses depending on the type of the disorder they have. Among boys with ADHD, they tend to become hyperactive. Girls with ADHD, on the other, are more likely to become distracted from what they were supposed to be doing.

Another difference between the two can be observed in the way a child processes information. Children with ADHD are characterized by their tendency to make impulsive decisions and their difficulty in acknowledging the consequences of the bad choices that they have made.

In comparison, highly sensitive children are incredibly conscientious and deliberate when it comes to making decisions. They usually take their time in analyzing the details they have on hand and then check it against their currently held attitudes, beliefs, and feelings about the matter. If it turns out that they have made the wrong decision, highly sensitive children would feel guilt and remorse about their mistake, especially if the effects of the wrong move have an impact on their ego or the welfare of the people around them.

Having Both

As you read this chapter, you might be picking up ideas that your highly sensitive child also may or may not have ADHD. While one of the goals of this chapter is to bring awareness about this possibility, it is much better to ask for the professional opinion of a child development expert before accepting or dismissing this thought.

Nowadays, various treatment options for children with ADHD are available. Some work more effectively for others, while some could have side effects that are too much for the child to handle in their day-to-day life. Given the complexities brought about by high sensitivity, it is essential to get the help of an expert before deciding how you are going to manage and meet your child's needs.

Chapter 7:
Sensory Food Aversions

Whether or not their children are highly sensitive, picky eating is a common problem faced by many parents. However, HSCs exhibit this to a greater degree. It is not just a matter of preference for them. In their case, these children have sensory food aversions, or also known as selective eating. Discover in this chapter what this means and why it is a tough challenge that both parents and their HSCs must overcome.

What is Sensory Food Aversion?

This refers to the overreaction of a person's senses when they eat certain types of food. It does not only involve their sense of taste though. It may also be triggered by the smell, texture, and temperature of the food.

The exact cause of sensory food aversion is still unknown to this day. However, some researchers point out that it is usually due to the inability to process too many stimuli that a person gets while they are eating.

Other than HSCs, children with ADHD, SPD, as well

as those who belong to the autism spectrum, tend to suffer from this condition, too. In their case, the most likely cause is the mouthfeel of the foods they are eating. For example, some children are fine with pureed carrots. However, the moment you try to feed them sliced carrots, they can no longer eat them.

Some instances of selective eating may be caused just by the appearance of the food. It may be the color, the presentation, the brand, or even the way it is packaged.

How could you tell if your child has a sensory food aversion? According to experts, the first signs are spitting out the food or completely refusing to take another bite. At some point, the child may start feeling nauseated or downright vomiting at the mere sight or smell of the food.

If this does not address properly, the child may exhibit these behaviors to other types of food that have similar qualities as the one they are originally averse to. For example, suppose he has developed an extreme dislike of carrots. In that case, he might become worried about eating squash or oranges because of the similarities of the foods in terms of color.

What If It Is Not a Case of Selective Eating?

Child development experts have noted that there are times when sensory aversion is not the cause of picky eating among children. Sometimes, it is a manifestation of issues related to their oral-motor abilities. This refers to the movements of the jaw and the tongue to chew and swallow food correctly.

If a child has oral-motor issues, they may exhibit similar behaviors associated with sensory food aversion. They will refuse to eat or spit out. Some also tend to gag or vomit when they try to process their food.

An obvious sign that your child is suffering from oral-motor problems and not selective eating is when they prefer to eat food that requires minimal mouth movements. For example, anything that can melt in their mouths without having to chew would be their preferred food.

Despite this sign, it is highly recommended to seek a professional opinion to determine the actual cause of your child's eating problem. Given their different natures, the treatment for sensory taste aversion and oral-motor issues are also different.

Regardless of which condition your child is suffering

from, you must take action immediately because thinking that these are just problems during mealtimes could blindside you of their effects on the nutritional intake and proper development of your child.

When Picky Eating Becomes a Bigger Issue

You and your child would face the following probable consequences of selective eating if it continues to be an unaddressed problem for too long:

- Less Diverse Diet
  Because your child refuses to eat certain types of food, their diet would become more and more restricted. Studies show that more children show aversion towards fruits, vegetables, and meats of all the food groups. These are excellent sources of the vitamins, minerals, and other nutrients that they need to grow and stay healthy, so continually refusing to eat them would snowball into a bigger problem later on. This could be further exacerbated by the tendency of children to prefer eating refined carbohydrates, which does not offer as much nutritional value as the other food groups.

- Nutritional Deficiencies

  Over time, the restricted diet of picky eaters would cause them to suffer from nutritional deficiencies, particularly of Vitamin C, Vitamin D, and protein. Aside from the obvious health concerns that this would pose to them, it could also make them lose weight to the point of becoming underweight for their size and age.

- Distress Among Other Family Members

  Mealtimes with the family would be a lot more stressful if one of the members is exhibiting the signs of sensory food aversion such as spitting, gagging, and vomiting. Furthermore, it would complicate the food preparation process for the caretakers of the home because they need to cater to the specific needs of the picky eater. Imagine how much trouble this would be if more than one child of your household suffers from this condition.

- Fear of Eating with Other People or Other Places

  Many highly sensitive children who have sensory food aversion become fearful about the idea of eating with others since they find it shameful for them. They also do not want to risk the chance of being misunderstood or offending others for refusing to eat certain types of food. Moreover, several picky eaters do not want to eat at other places because of the thought of having to face the food they are averse to.

Though the research about treatment for sensory food aversions is minimal, some child development experts recommend techniques and therapy methods that could be effective for highly sensitive children. The specific ways of handling the sensory food aversions of your child will be discussed further in the latter part of this book.

Part 2:

Parenting Strategies That Will Help Your Highly Sensitive Child Thrive

Chapter 8:
Hidden Benefits of Being Highly Sensitive

Before thinking of ways on how to guide and nurture your highly sensitive child, reflect first on how you view high sensitivity as a natural part of your child's personality. Do you see it as a burden for you and your child? Or perhaps an issue that you must resolve?

Such negative views about high sensitivity may be rooted in the perception of your culture or society. Researchers have noted that some think of sensitivity as a sign of weakness, especially among men. Certain behaviors associated with this trait, such as crying easily and throwing a tantrum, are also viewed as unpleasant—thus further stigmatizing high sensitivity.

To achieve your goal of helping your highly sensitive child to thrive as an individual, you and your child must shift this kind of view and regard this trait as a gift and an opportunity instead. Read through the list below to learn more about the hidden benefits that the high sensitivity trait can give to your child.

A highly sensitive person finds happiness and satisfaction in the simple things in life.

HSPs do not need or ask for much to feel joy. They like going for walks on their own, especially during the times of the day where there are only a few people out and they can observe their surroundings in peace. Even just have a nice, hot bath while reading their favorite book could make HSPs forget about the stressful day they have had. Such simple pleasures are easy to do and get, so HSPs can get access to moments of pure happiness without having to spend so much money, time, or effort.

A highly sensitive person can be a good judge of character.

Being good at reading people comes naturally for HSPs. Aside from being able to notice tiny details, such as how a person ties their shoes or what kind of coffee someone likes to drink, they are also good observers when it comes to non-verbal cues, such as facial expressions, body posture, and hand gestures. They also pay attention to what makes others laugh, frown, or raise their eyebrows.

Their brain combines these various bits of information to form a general opinion about whether or not they should approach or befriend someone—and more often than not, their opinion about a person's character tends to be accurate.

A highly sensitive person can spot connections that others might miss.

Due to their high sensitivity, these people process information differently. Rather than focusing solely on the facts given to them, they can form connections that usually turn out to be accurate. Though they may have a hard time when faced with a lot of details to remember, they can understand the core of the matter, which then allows them to come up with ideas and conclusions that are out of the box.

A highly sensitive person feels pleasant sensations to a much greater degree.

The senses of HSPs are naturally heightened, so they feel things more intensely than most people do. This poses a problem when it comes to negative stimuli, but it also enables them to get more pleasure when they sense something pleasant or appealing to them. For example, many HSPs are sensitive to touch and texture. Therefore, they get more joy out of being wrapped in their favorite blanket, as well as being hugged by their loved ones. Those who are sensitive to visual stimuli would feel greatly moved by simply looking at paintings or watching live performances.

A highly sensitive person does not feel dependent on caffeine, alcohol, or pain medication.

The high sensitivity of these individuals does not only affect their senses but also how their body reacts to the things they eat and drink. They react strongly to small doses, so they do not feel the need to imbibe a lot of coffee to feel more awake in the morning. They tend to be light drinkers too, even if they are just drinking red wine. When in pain, they rarely need strong medication because a simple aspirin can easily relieve them of their aches and pains. Because of their high sensitivity, most

HSPs save a lot of money while also keeping themselves healthier and free from substance dependency.

A highly sensitive person can do well at activities that require excellent fine-motor movements.

HSPs are excellent at controlling their body movements. They can hold still for longer periods, and they make it a point to avoid making a mistake. As such, highly sensitive people can become accomplished in certain activities that require fine motor movements, such as drawing, sewing, pottery making, and playing string or wind musical instruments.

A highly sensitive person learns new languages better.

This hidden benefit also stems from HSPs' ability to form connections in the information they are processing. Learning a new language is not just memorizing new vocabulary. It also involves understanding their meaning and which kinds of context the words should be used. Though HSPs may take more time in learning these aspects of the new language they are adapting to, they tend to be better at applying what they have learned in practical situations and conversations.

A highly sensitive person is in touch with their spirituality.

Many HSPs find it easy to tap into their spiritual side. Depending on their culture, they tend to show commitment to religious activities, like reading sacred texts or attending religious services. This does not automatically mean that HSPs are just good at following organized religions. They are also naturally inclined to practices that require them to open their minds beyond physical reality. Their minds are capable of reflecting on the probable answers to deep questions about humanity, ethics, as well as various ideas and theories that do not agree with a simple black-or-white mentality.

It is quite easy for HSPs and those around them to focus on the limitations imposed upon them by this trait. However, focusing solely on that side would prevent the HSP from living up to their potential and enjoying a good life. Give your highly sensitive child a chance to accomplish this by reminding them regularly of the positive aspects of their personality and helping them harness the hidden benefits of being highly sensitive.

Chapter 9:
The Special Connection Between Highly Sensitive Children and Animals

One of the many gifts of being highly sensitive is the ability to forge a strong and deep bond with animals. Children, in particular, benefit greatly from this because of the many learning opportunities that it could provide. Because of this, experts suggest to parents of HSCs to bring in a pet to their family—or at least allow their children to be regularly exposed to animals.

To better understand this recommendation, let's discuss why highly sensitive children have a special connection with animals and how you could guide your child into learning the life lessons and skills that could be gained by bonding with animals.

High Sensitivity and Animals

According to Dr. Aron, highly sensitive children find it easy and almost natural to form a special relationship with animals. These children have heightened responsiveness towards emotions, thus enabling them to connect with animals on a different level than those with lower sensitivity.

Several animals possess high intelligence that may be observed in their ability to follow instructions, make sound decisions, and express emotions. They also tend to have sharper senses that could detect stimuli that are far too subtle for an average human. With these qualities, it should not come as a surprise why highly sensitive individuals can understand and strongly empathize with not just their pets but even animals found in the wild.

This connection becomes more profound when highly sensitive children see animals that are in distress. An urge to help or relieve the animal from pain or stress may felt so deeply that they are almost always moved to action. They can also read the mood and even health condition of animals, mainly if it is their pet.

Much like connecting with other people, these kids benefit from interacting with animals. Studies show that it can be a great source of support for highly sensitive children, especially when they feel overwhelmed. Even if they cannot communicate through verbal means, these children and their respective pets could gain an understanding of one another on a deeper level.

Though animals, in general, have a positive effect among highly sensitive children, certain types are known for being easier to bond with—for example, dogs, cats, birds, rabbits, and horses. These may be domesticated and kept as pets, thus giving more chances for the child to grow and learn valuable life skills through them.

Learning Opportunities

Bonding with animals can be quite beneficial for HSCs, especially in terms of what they can learn from doing so. For example, through animals, your child will learn about:

- Unconditional love and pure emotions
  Unlike humans, animals are capable of show-ing love and care without expectations. If a dog feels excited about the prospect of going to the dog park, your highly sensitive child may be able to observe how pure joy looks like—no-frills, no unreasonable conditions, and no hid-den agenda.
- How companionship may come in different forms

If your child needs someone who could stay by their side whenever they feel overstimulated or just plain tired, animals are suitable options for them. Letting your HSC take comfort in the company of their pets would teach them that their social relationships are not limited to other people but also to the animals that they will take care of and grow to love.

- Resilience in the face of uncontrollable things

  Many things in life are beyond one's control. HSCs tend to feel bad even if they really cannot do anything about it. On the other hand, animals are incredibly resilient when it comes to similar scenarios. Failures do not take them down hard and for too long. They mourn their loss and then move on. Your HSC could learn from this kind of attitude and behaviors and exhibit more resiliency in their day-to-day life.

- Living in the moment

  Animals are usually not burdened with thoughts about what happened to them in the past or what could happen to them in the future. They recognize and appreciate what is going on in the present and become excited at what would likely happen soon. Highly sensitive children tend to get caught up in their thoughts and reflections that they may fail to see what is going on around them. Learning how to stay connected to their reality and live life one second at a time may be possible for HSCs if they continually bond and observe the animals around them.

- New perspectives

  HSCs have naturally high levels of empathy. This does not only apply to other people but also animals. Observing and bonding with animals would teach them what the world looks like from different perspectives. It widens their understanding of their surroundings and enables them to be more compassionate and considerate of the needs and wants of those who cannot speak to them.

- Different ways to de-stress

  Spending time with animals can be a soothing activity for HSCs. For example, taking the dog out for a hike could allow your child to feel more connected with nature. Bird watching in silence may also be a good way to relax and relieve themselves of the stresses they had throughout the day.

Eventually, a child who grew up while having a special bond with animals would be more open about pursuing career opportunities that involve animals. Though not every animal-related jobs are suitable for HSPs, there are somewhere they can harness the strengths brought about by their high sensitivity. These include careers like becoming an animal trainer, groomer, or sitter. Their deep understanding and genuine concern for animals would enable them to excel in the said fields.

What if your current lifestyle doesn't allow you to have a pet? Some do not have a space large enough to accommodate an extra animal in their homes, while others are prohibited from bringing in one because of the building rules.

If this is the case for you, consider joining an animal care volunteer program with your child. By doing so, your kid can interact and bond with animals without having to take them home as pets.

Chapter 10:
Highly Sensitive Introvert vs. Extrovert

For many people, the lines are blurred when it comes to identifying an introvert from a highly sensitive introvert. Several overlaps exist between the two, so it is understandable why differentiating one from the other can be confusing.

Matters become more complicated when it comes to an understanding of what it means to be a highly sensitive person because some consider themselves extroverts. At first glance, it may seem like the two traits cannot be possessed by the same person, but as you will learn later on in this chapter, this kind of HSP does exist. Your child might even be one of them.

Find out more about these different aspects of an HSP's personality in the following sections.

Introverts vs. Highly Sensitive Introverts

Because of how media portray introversion, many assume that it is synonymous with being quiet and unsociable. However, this is inaccurate because studies show that a lot of introverts like spending time with one or two close friends. Unlike their extroverted counterparts though, they become tired faster during social situations. This requires them to have lots of alone time, such as staying in the comforts of their home where they could recover and recharge their energy.

Researchers have found out that introversion is a genetic trait, and those who possess it have lower thresholds for the so-called "reward" chemical: dopamine. As a result, they feel satisfied doing things that are not too energetic or exciting, like reading or drawing. They become drained when they have to engage in social or intense activities like attending a big gathering or trying out a new team sport.

The majority of highly sensitive people are also introverted. This causes the misunderstanding that they are the same. However, an introverted person without the high sensitivity trait also exists. They do not exhibit the common qualities associated with HSPs, such as deep emotional processing and strong observational skills. These people do not read people as accurately as HSPs do, but they also do not feel as greatly affected by the stimulation they receive from others and their environment.

Qualities of a Highly Sensitive Extrovert

Usually, HSPs are neither sociable nor talkative. They prefer to stay in their corner while observing others and running through their thoughts and ideas in silence. Loud and adrenaline-filled activities tend to turn them off since it could lead them to feel over-stimulated.

These characteristics, however, do not apply to all highly sensitive individuals. According to experts, there are also highly sensitive extroverts who thrive in the company of other people and willingly joins exciting events. Though it may seem like they are a walking contradiction, this type of HSPs faces a big challenge of balancing their need to socialize with their limitations when it comes to processing too much sensory information at the same time.

As you know by now, about 20% of the total population possesses the high sensitivity trait. Of these, only 30% fall under the extroverted side of the spectrum. Because of their rarity, many people often misunderstand what it means to be a highly sensitive extrovert.

To find out if an HSP is also an extrovert, check if they exhibit the following signs:

1. They use their keen observational skills to improve their relationships with other people.

   Because of their high sensitivity, HSE notices small or subtle details that most tend to miss. Using this knowledge, they make thoughtful remarks or gestures, such as praising someone for learning a new makeup technique or giving gifts that bear the recipient's favorite color.

   HSEs are also considered as good listeners by their family, friends, and even co-workers. They pay attention to what others have to say, and they reflect deeply about the information they get. They are also known for giving wise advice that makes them seem like they are older than their actual age.

2. They enjoy working as part of a group.

   Yes, highly sensitive introverts can be good team players, too. However, they do their best work; they are left on their own to focus better on their task. On the other hand, HSEs actively look for opportunities to collaborate with others on their activities and projects. They enjoy trading ideas and helping others, although they can only do so in limited amounts of time.

84

3. They have a tight-knit group of friends.

    Unlike other types of extroverts, HSEs still prefer to form deep relationships rather than make a lot of new but casual ones. While they may also have a relatively large network of social connections, their true friends tend to be small in number. After all, they are excellent judges of character so they can figure out which one of these people understands and accepts them for who they are.

4. They cannot spend too much time alone or with other people.

    Another contradiction that HSE embodies is their craving for both some downtime on their own and having someone they could talk to. The key is to balance these two so that they would feel happy and fulfilled without risking the possibility of becoming overstimulated. Furthermore, if they spend too much time on their own, they would start feeling incredibly lonely and bored.

5. They like doing traditional social activities on their own.

    Activities such as eating at a restaurant or going to the cinema are group activities for most people. HSEs, in comparison, do not find it odd if they want to do those same activities without the company of their family, friends, or colleagues. They consider these as outings as something that is specially reserved for themselves, wherein they can explore new places and try out new things along the way.

6. They look forward to having new experiences.

    Their high sensitivity trait makes them suitable for following routines, but once in a while, HSEs also want to inject something different into their day-to-day lives. It can range from tiny changes in their lunch for that day, or something as big as going on a vacation at a place where they have not been to before. Yes, they would need more time to get used to these novel experiences but they would get a wave of positive emotions that make everything worth their time and effort.

7. They can suddenly feel exhausted while socializing or doing something new.

    Highly sensitive extroverts might seem like they can do everything that regular extroverts could, but they can only last for a much shorter period. After all, their systems are processing a lot of sensory information, so at some point, they would feel themselves crashing down to the point of needing time to recharge on their own. Much like other HSPs, they have to do this somewhere that is quiet and away from other people. Once they have regained their vigor though, they would likely seek again for quality social interactions or trying out an activity that they have not experienced before.

Knowing the difference between highly sensitive introverts and highly sensitive extroverts could help you better understand the various aspects of your child's personality. Regardless of where your child falls in this spectrum though, what's important is for you to teach them how to appreciate and accept all facets of their being, learn to harness their strengths, and respect their limitations.

ELENA JENKINS

Chapter 11:
Common Challenges of Raising
a Highly Sensitive Child

Sensory processing sensitivity can cause some issues to the day-to-day life of your child. It may manifest in various forms, and one child can be sensitive in more than one way. In this chapter, let's go over the different types of sensitivities that your child might have and how you could effectively help them manage or even get over their issues.

Sensitivity to Sounds

Many people do not think the background music of an action-filled video game or the barking of a nearby dog is bothersome or unbearable. On the other hand, highly sensitive kids find such noises hard to manage—sometimes to the point of overwhelming their senses completely. This effect on them may be taken up a notch further if they hear unexpected sounds, such as the fire alarm suddenly going off.

Since you cannot simply prevent these kinds of

sounds from interfering with your child's day-to-day life, the right way to handle this is by first gaining an understanding of your child's limits when it comes to various types of sound. You can then use this information as a basis for setting the limits and strategies for the welfare of your child.

Going by the examples given earlier, if your child exhibits sensitivity towards the background music of their favorite video games, you can bring their attention to it and suggest turning down the volume whenever they play.

Unfortunately, not every sound can be controlled this way, especially when your child is outside your home. To help you and your child better manage situations that could trigger them, here are some helpful tips to keep in mind:

1. Inform others about your child's hearing sensitivity.

    You do not have to bear solely the responsibility of keeping your highly sensitive child safe and comfortable. Protecting your child could be a team effort by the adults around them, such as other family members, neighbors, your friends, and their teachers.

Let them know about your child's limitations when it comes to certain sounds, and explain to them what must be done if your child encounters the said sounds or if your child becomes overwhelmed from too many auditory stimuli in their environment. In this way, others would be able to guide and take care properly of your highly sensitive child, even when you are not around.

2. Protect your child's ears.

    Nowadays, some manufacturers offer noise-canceling earphones, headphones, or earplugs that are suitable for children. Get one for your highly sensitive child so that they can muffle loud noises that cannot be avoided or turned off. Just make sure that the device does not completely block off every sound because it might pose some serious safety risks to your child.

3. Try putting on some background noise.

    According to studies, background noise, such as the buzzing of an electric fan or the television on low volume, can help lessen the impact of loud or shocking noises that may overwhelm your child. Consider using a white noise machine as well, especially when your child sleeps or naps. This could help improve the quality of their sleep since it could keep sudden noises from waking them up.

4. Plan in case your child is going to a crowded place.

   To do this, do some research about the place that your child will be going to. Check out when the peak times are, as well as what kind of noises your child should expect to hear. Arming yourself and your child with this knowledge would enable you to come up with a plan on how to minimize their effect or avoid the probable triggers for their sound sensitivity altogether.

5. Always prioritize your child's safety.

   Emergencies usually entail sounding off alarms or sirens that could easily overwhelm a highly sensitive child. Turning off these safety and security signals is not an option for obvious reasons. What you can do instead is to minimize your child's exposure to them as much as possible.

For example, take the initiative to teach your child what they should do in case the fire alarm goes off. Doing so would prevent your child from panicking or staying clueless when they hear this loud noise. Instead, it would prompt them to find an exit or get away from the burning immediately, thus reducing their probability of being overwhelmed by the sound of the alarm.

Schools also conduct fire drills regularly. In this case, inform the teacher ahead of time about your child's sensitivity towards the fire alarm. In that way, the teacher may be able to seat your child near the door so that they can leave the classroom properly but quickly when the fire drill starts.

Sensitivity to Sight

Can your child be near bright sources of light? Do they complain whenever they see flashing lights around them? Are they frequently requesting for you to turn down the brightness of their devices or wear sunglasses while they are outside?

If such scenarios sound familiar to you, then your child is likely sensitive to visual stimuli. This can affect them not only physically but also in terms of their academic performance and ability to fall asleep.

Fortunately, there are various ways on how you can help address the challenges brought about by visual sensitivity:

1. Change the kind of lighting you have at home.

   Look for light bulbs that give off a soothing glow. Nowadays, there are colored bulbs that emit soft lighting, too.

   Consider changing your light switches into dimmers instead so that you can directly adjust the brightness. For your child's room, get them a night light or an adjustable lamp so that your child would have an option in case they find the overhead lighting to be too bright for them.

2. Limit their exposure to bright lights, sunlight, and glare while they are outside.

   At home, you can easily modify the lighting

to suit your child. However, when they are outside, there are only some things that you can do to protect them from being irritated or overwhelmed by bright or flashing lights.

One of the easiest ways is always to pack a pair of sunglasses for your child. Have it on hand in your bag or somewhere in your car so that your child can ask for them whenever they need to. Remember to get your car windows tinted in a dark shade as well.

At school, discuss with your child's teacher about the possibility of moving them away from the windows, especially if sunlight streams through them. Offer to donate some curtains or blinds for the windows, if need be.

3. Opt for less flashy colors.

    Some HSCs cannot stand bright colors, especially neon ones. Avoid buying items for them that are in those shades of colors. In case that your home has decors, painted walls, or carpets that are brightly colored, look for a replacement to make your child more comfortable.

4. Minimize the visual clutter around your child.

   Visual clutter may be in the form of having too many objects around them or exposing them to design patterns that are too "busy" or contrasting. To resolve this, rope in everyone living in your home to keep things neat and tidy. Please encourage them to put things back in their correct places after use.

   For your child's bedroom, avoid putting up many posters on their wall—no matter if they are decorative or educational. Teach your child to put away their toys, books, and other knickknacks before they go to sleep.

Sensitivity to Touch

Touch sensitivity among children can be mostly observed based on their reaction towards their clothes, the temperature, and pain. The first thing that you should keep in mind if your child exhibits this is that they are not needlessly tricky. Highly sensitive children are hardwired to feel stimuli on a level wherein something that does not typically bother you is going to make them feel irritated, annoyed, or overwhelmed.

Fortunately, there are various ways on how you could address issues like this. Below are helpful tips that you could try doing to help your highly sensitive kid overcome the challenges associated with touch sensitivity:

1. Allow your child to choose their clothes.

    Start by giving them an option about the clothes they want to wear the next day. Studies show doing so would make it easier for parents to get their children dressed.

    In case that they have to go to a special event with a dress code, pick at least three outfit combinations for them, and give them the freedom to select the final choice among your shortlist. You can also try just giving them a basic idea of what kind of clothes must be worn, and wait until they have decided on their final outfit choice.

2. Let your child try on clothes he/she would wear at least the night before.

    Ask your child to try on the clothes they

have picked. Check with them if there is anything that they wish to change and if they feel comfortable. Testing clothes in advance would ensure that your child's touch sensitivity will not cause any problem on the day itself.

3. Give your child time to get used to their clothes.

    Avoid rushing your child when it comes to picking their clothes. It could just make them feel more stressed and eventually lead to an outburst. Refrain from rushing your child when they are trying their clothes on, too. HSCs need time to process how they feel. Allow them enough time and space to decide if what they are wearing is not too tight or scratchy against their skin.

4. Buy more comfortable clothing for your children.

    Look for clothes that are made of naturally soft fabrics, such as cotton and wool. Avoid getting them anything that has tight collars. If their clothes have tags on them, remove those since they can be irritating to the skin.

5. Give your child advice on what to wear depending on the weather.

   HSCs may be sensitive to temperature. As such, what they choose to wear can trigger their touch sensitivity in case the temperature suddenly changes. For example, rather than a thick woolen sweater, explain to them that a jacket might be a better choice since they can just easily take it off if it becomes too hot for them. Similarly, tell them how packing a scarf in their schoolbag could be useful to them later on if they suddenly feel cold while at school.

Aside from texture and temperature, touch sensitivity may be in the form of an overreaction towards pain. Due to their deeper sensory processing, the pain from simple cuts, scratches, bruises, or accidental bumps may become magnified to the point of extreme discomfort.

If your child experiences this kind of sensitivity, do not attempt to downplay how they feel. It might seem like a trivial matter that can be resolved without going to the hospital, but the pain they feel is valid for your child. This unpleasant sensation may be even more exacerbated by their tendency to blame themselves for making the mistake that ends up hurting them—regardless if it is truly their fault or if it is just an accident.

What you can do is teach your child how to properly manage this kind of pain. Provided that it is not a life-threatening injury, your child could just practice calming techniques that will prevent their feelings from escalating into a full-blown meltdown. Then, tell them that they should feel free to seek the attention of someone who could administer first aid to them. It could be you, some other member of the family, or their teachers when they are at school.

Consider enrolling them in first-aid classes when they are older, too. If they can handle the pressure involved, anyone will benefit from learning how to conduct first aid for themselves and others.

Sensitivity to Taste

Many highly sensitive kids are labeled as picky eaters. The thing is, this goes beyond mere preferences about their food. These children process taste-related stimuli on a different level so they can be easily affected by the taste and texture of food and whatever else they put inside their mouth, such as toothpaste and medicine.

Some parents think that they can keep their highly sensitive children sated and happy by just refraining from giving the children the tastes they dislike. However, this may pose a big problem if the children would not get the right amount of nutrients from their food.

As such, parents need to figure out a good way to manage the taste sensitivity of their children without having to force them into eating foods that make them unhappy or uncomfortable. Check out the tips below that could help you get started on this:

1. Observe your child's reaction to different kinds of food.

    In general, reactions to certain food remain consistent, especially if it is particularly strong. However, various factors could affect how your highly sensitive child perceives the food they eat. For example, if they do not get enough sleep the previous night, they might not want to drink the cup of warm milk that they usually have for breakfast. In such cases, the aspect that must be addressed is not the food itself but rather the circumstances that led your child into refusing milk.

Merely observing your child is not enough, however. Keep track of your child's reactions for at least a week, and then write down what you have seen in a journal. Make sure to note down any probable patterns that you have observed since those could help you later on in preventing troubles with your child's taste sensitivity.

2. Slowly introduce your child to new types of food.

There are two important things to remember when introducing something new to highly sensitive kids: Do it one at a time and ask them to try just a tiny bit first.

Presenting too many new food items at a single meal or in quick succession to your child would likely overwhelm them. Doing so may also keep you from observing their reaction towards the new food. Furthermore, studies show that it takes up to 10 to 15 "taste tests" before a child could decide if they want a particular food or not. Going slowly would give them enough time to process the food that you are introducing into their diet.

One effective technique used by occupational therapists for taste-sensitive children is called the "snake test." You can try doing this on your own through these steps:

a. Allow your child to familiarize himself/herself with the new food.

Your goal at this point is to get your child to handle the food without feeling uncomfortable or disgusted. At first, they can just look at the food. Then after some time, try to get them to smell or touch the food.

b. Encourage your child to taste a bit of the new food.

This does not have to be a small bite. During the initial stages, a quick lick of the food would suffice. Then, slowly work up your way by increasing the duration of the lick until the child feels ready to take a bite and swallow the food. Depending on the child's level of sensitivity, this step may take several weeks or even months before the child completely accepts the new food.

3. Establish your child's food-related limits and preferences.

Make sure that both you and your child agree upon the limits on what he/she would eat, as well as his/her willingness to try out new food. Forcing your child to go beyond will be counterintuitive and might even cause resentment and distrust between the two of you. Share with your child your observations about their eating patterns and what you plan to do next in terms of introducing more food into their diet. Doing so would increase your chances of getting their cooperation and fostering a deeper bond with them.

4. Be creative.

Go the extra mile by presenting meals and snacks in different ways to your child. Just because your child did not like fresh strawberries, it does not automatically mean that they will also not like a strawberry smoothie. In such cases, the issue is not the taste but rather the texture of the food. Experiment with the recipes using similar ingredients to discover which ones your highly sensitive child would like.

Sensitivity to certain types of food does involve not only the sense of taste, but also the sense of smell. Therefore, you can help your highly sensitive child manage their preferences by understanding first the connection between the two. Failing to do so might blindside you from potentially triggering stimuli that your child's nose could pick up.

The tongue can detect if the food stimuli taste sweet, sour, bitter, savory, or salty. While that alone could determine whether or not your child would eat the food, their sense of smell could provide more input that may either encourage them to eat anyway or to become even more averse towards the food.

For example, your child enjoys eating sweets, but she cannot stand tangy smells like citrus fruits. Because of this, she would likely refuse to eat fresh orange slices or have a sip of lemonade.

Your child might also refuse to eat something because the smell of the area where they are eating overwhelms them. Because of this, some parents set up eating areas that are free from strong odors, such as air fresheners, to keep such smells from affecting their children's mealtimes.

Other than hypersensitivity, another common challenge faced by HSCs is anxiety. Take note, however, that your child's anxiety may be a side-effect of their bad experiences when it comes to their sensitivities. For example, if they frequently get headaches at school because they are seated near the window, your child would start feeling anxious about the idea of going to school. Similarly, mealtimes may become a tense affair for them if you continue to serve something that could make them gag or vomit.

As their parents, it is your responsibility to calm these worries and fears, especially since your inaction may lead them to develop more serious anxiety disorders in the future. Fortunately, managing your child's anxiety, especially if during its initial stages, can be done even without seeking the help of a therapist. For example, many parents are now more open to teaching their children about various calming and relaxation techniques like breathing exercises, meditation, and yoga for kids.

Teaching coping techniques to your child would also be helpful, particularly in taking their mind away from what is worrying them. Inspire positive feelings within your child by understanding what makes them smile or laugh. Observe which activities they find fun, and let them engage in those activities whenever they feel anxious. Studies also show that the mere act of smiling could also make people start feeling better even if they are smiling for no specific reason at all.

However, if your child has already developed severe anxiety, do not hesitate to look for a qualified therapist who preferably specializes in handling highly sensitive children.

The key in addressing the above-given challenges is open communication between you and HSC about their experiences and feelings. Reassure them that you are there to help them overcome these difficulties so that they can focus more on developing their talents, skills, and relationships.

Chapter 12:
Discipline Strategies to Use with Highly Sensitive Children

Raising well-adjusted kids involves disciplining them when needed. This could pose some challenges for parents of highly sensitive children because of their natural tendency to feel things deeper. What works for other kids or your other offspring does not automatically mean that it would be as effective or beneficial for your HSC.

Moreover, disciplining children with high sensitivity could send the wrong message if you dole out punishments for something that is beyond their control. For example, HSCs may cry uncontrollably when they feel overwhelmed or if they are in the middle of a sensory breakdown. Disciplining them for crying out in public is a bad move. Rather than punishment, highly sensitive children need to be given time and space to recover from being overstimulated.

Some parents who do not fully understand high sensitivity may also think that the shy or timid nature of their children could be "phased out" if they discipline them for not listening to their advice to be more pro-active or sociable. Aside from the problem of misla-beling HSCs, this kind of attitude would only further increase the children's fear and doubts when it comes to interacting with other people.

Being strict with highly sensitive children may be helpful in some ways, but being harsh is completely another thing. Again, these kids feel things on another level. Others may find the discipline strategy to be tol-erable, but there is no guarantee that your child would also feel the same way.

Here are some examples of discipline strategies that have been observed by experts to be ineffective among HSCs:

a. Isolation
    Many parents' go-to discipline method is to send their kids to their room. They assume that children would use this timeout to reflect on what they did wrong and come up with an apology and promises to be better. This would also serve as a punishment because usually, the kids would be in their room without their preferred means of entertainment, such as their computer or mobile devices.

b. Yelling

Many parents tend to yell at their kids when they have been disobeyed or disrespected. Some do it deliberately to show their anger or displeasure, while some say that they raise their voice unintentionally, wherein they could not control themselves well enough to refrain from doing so.

Yelling is bad enough for children who are not highly sensitive. Imagine how much more harmful it is for HSCs, who are known for being incredibly conscious of non-verbal cues, including the tone and volume of one's voice.

When yelled at, highly sensitive children are likely going to be scared of you and might even cause them to resent you. The loud volume could also lead to overstimulation, which would then further prevent them from understanding what you are saying at that moment. As a result, the purpose of your yelling will be defeated since the child only knows that you are upset at them—not why you are yelling or what they could do better next time.

c. Withholding

One of the common fears among highly sensitive children is losing their parents' love because of their thoughts and behaviors. Being too harsh on their punishment while also maintaining a cold attitude towards them would make them believe that you no longer care or love them.

HSCs thrive better when they are treated gently. Letting them stew over their worries that they have lost your affection and support would prevent them from learning the lessons they should reflect on instead.

d. Shaming

Because of HSC's tendency to personally feel responsible for their mistakes, they are known for trying hard to abide by the rules and follow instructions. As a result, when they fail to do so, they feel extremely bad about it and blame themselves for messing things up, regardless of the actual cause. They do not need more finger-pointing or insults from the people around them because they are already beating themselves up for it.

Questioning harshly why they failed could also be a dire hit for them. Being called out for their sensitivity about the matter would also make them feel even worse. In the end, rather than toughening up your child's character, you would only demotivate them from trying again.

Rather than the above-given methods, here are eight strategies that you should keep in mind to help you figure out the best way to properly instill discipline in your highly sensitive child:

Strategy No. 1: Set up a place in your home where your child can decompress.

This is the same as sending your child away to their room. Instead of isolating them, the goal here is to provide a space where they could calm down their thoughts and emotions. Disciplining them while they are emotional or overstimulated would just be a waste of your time and efforts.

What distinguishes this from the usual timeout corner is that it should not be seen as a punishment. You are not going to take away their favorite toys or books from them. This spot should have the essential things that would make them feel comfortable, such as soft pillows and blankets and a plushy arm-chair. If your child finds music to be soothing, consider playing those songs in the background as well.

This could be an easy thing to set up in your home. However, what should you do if your child requires to be disciplined while both of you are out of the house?

In such cases, control yourself and refrain from disciplining them in public. Doing so would only greatly embarrass your HSC, which could then make them feel more emotional about their mistake or misbehavior. Remind them, however, that you would talk about this later when both of you are at home so that they would be aware of any wrongdoing that they have done.

If their emotions become out of control while you are still in public, lead your child to a quiet spot away from other people. Take note of your current mood and actions too, since those could be the factors that are aggravating the situation.

Strategy No. 2: Practice empathy.

HSCs respond better to disciplinary actions if they feel that their parents understand what made them act out in the first place. Give them time to explain themselves and listen well to their words and what goes on in between the lines. Avoid jumping to conclusions based on your assumptions and observations.

To show that you understand them, say back how they felt in your own words. You should also try to paraphrase their explanation to prove that you have listened carefully. Knowing that you are both on the same page would convince them that what you have to say next addresses their concerns and are being told with good intentions.

Strategy No. 3: Pay attention to your non-verbal cues.

By nature, highly sensitive children are sharp when it comes to reading the facial expressions, body gestures, and the tone and volume of the voice of the people around them. If they notice that yours are denoting anger and frustration, then they would likely feel more upset. They also start to ignore what you are saying at the moment because their focus has been caught on trying to process the meaning of your tone or body language.

Much like your child, you also need time to calm down first before attempting to discipline them. Aim to control your non-verbal cues while also showing that you are serious and firm about your words.

Strategy No. 4: Let your child know of your expectations and the consequences of their actions.

Since HSCs prefer knowing the expectations that others have on them, take the time to communicate how you want them to behave, especially when both of you are heading out to somewhere new. Explain to them why you are setting these rules and boundaries and the importance of following them. Make sure to check if they truly understand what you are saying. End this talk by specifying what will happen if they do not meet your expectations or break the rules you have agreed upon.

Do not assume that your child would remember everything you said right away. Remind them of these expectations and consequences regularly. For example, upon arriving at your destination during a family outing, you should spend a few minutes rehashing what they can do or cannot do once they have gotten out of the van. If they have any questions, answer them clearly but in as few words as possible so that they would remember what you said. Then, ask one more time if they understand everything before letting them go. Doing this would lessen the chances that HSCs would misbehave.

Strategy No. 5: Kneel or sit down in front of your child.

Getting down to your child's level by sitting down or kneeling would help you connect better even when disciplining them. It shows them that you are willing to listen to them and understand what had happened. It also makes them feel safe and reassured that you still care about them despite their wrongdoing.

Strategy No. 6: Reassure your child that you still love them.

As explained earlier in this chapter, highly sensitive kids need to know that their parents love them even after being disciplined. You can do this once they have fulfilled the consequences. Start by hugging them and then praising them for listening to you. Spend some time together while talking about their thoughts and feelings at the moment. Answer any doubts or confusion that they may have, and reiterate the important lessons they should always keep in mind.

As with any other parenting strategy, you need to be consistent with the way you discipline your child. Otherwise, you would send mixed signals to your highly sensitive child, which could then prevent them from learning from your attempts to discipline them.

Some of these strategies might not come naturally to you—for example, paying attention to how loud you speak. However, with enough practice and dedication to parenting your HSC the right way, you would eventually be able to turn such behaviors into one of your habits.

Remember that these strategies are not guaranteed to work for every highly sensitive child. Each of them is unique and requires the understanding and acceptance of their parents.

What you have decided now to be part of your disciplining style is also not set in stone. This means that you can change how you discipline your child depending on how well they react to the strategies you use on them. Furthermore, you might have to adjust your style as they grow older and gain more experiences from outside your home.

Chapter 13:
Ways to Help Your HSC Develop High Confidence

Many highly sensitive children encounter challenges that require self-confidence. Whether it is many new friends or performing an unfamiliar task, HSCs worry about the potential embarrassment that could arise from the situation and about the reactions of those who would witness their actions.

To help your child overcome their issues and build their self-confidence, here are seven tips that are both doable and effective:

1. Assure your child that high sensitivity is a normal and natural trait to have. Many HSCs tend to notice that they are different from the other kids around them even at an early age. This may be even more conspicuous if they believe that they are the only ones who hesitate to try out the new monkey bars in the playground or if they feel really scared about the group performance at school.

    Failing to address this matter would not only

warp your child's attitude and beliefs about high sensitivity but also further prevent them from building their self-confidence. What you can do is to explain to your child how high sensitivity is a trait that around 1 in 5 people possess. This means that among their friends and peers, there is a good chance that there are other highly sensitive kids as well.

Then, make sure to highlight the positive attributes that are associated with this trait. Through this, they would be able to see themselves in a much better light, despite the challenges and shortcomings brought about by high sensitivity. This would enable them to gain more confidence in their inherent qualities, talents, and learning abilities in the long run.

2. Actively listen to what your child has to say.

Showing interest in the thoughts and ideas of your child could boost their confidence. Kids who are often interrupted while speaking or needlessly criticized upon speaking their minds have a much harder time learning how to trust and believe in themselves.

This does not mean that you have to agree

with everything they have to say though. Listen well to their words, and share with them your thoughts about what you have heard. Praise good ideas and sentiments. When it comes to poor ones, explain to your child why you do not agree with their idea or thought, and show them how they could improve upon the idea or shift their thoughts for the better. Building the self-confidence of your highly sensitive child require conversations that are focused, open, and honest.

3. Be a role model for your child.

One of the first teachers your child would have is you. They will watch how you talk and behave and try to model themselves after you—deliberately or subconsciously. As such, if you are shy or easily intimidated, then your highly sensitive child would surely notice as well.

Developing self-confidence all of a sudden is an impossible feat to achieve. You can push yourself out of your comfort zone at your own pace, but in the meantime, try to, at least, look like you are self-confident.

Body language experts offer several tips on the behavioral mannerisms of confident people.

Common examples include standing straight and making eye contact when talking with others. Practice these behaviors until it feels natural for you to them. As you do so, your highly sensitive child would take note and most likely mimic your actions that show you are a confident individual.

4. Teach them about self-motivation and positivity despite failures.

   According to psychologist and author Dr. Carl Pickhardt, you can help your child build confidence by teaching them the habit of saying these three remarks:

   a. "I can do it."

      This sentence improves their perception of their skills and talents. Over time, children who say this when met with a challenge would believe more in themselves.

   b. "I want to make an effort."

      Motivation may come from an external factor or from within. This sentence focuses on the latter since self-confidence requires the ability to motivate one's self despite the difficulty or unpleasantness of the circumstances you are facing.

c. "I will give it a good try."

Through this statement, your child would learn that it is not just about starting something. It is also about giving their best shot to achieve the outcome that they want.

Confidence does not guarantee success, however. That is why your child needs to learn about the proper and healthy way to handle failures. Highly sensitive children in particular have a hard time processing mistakes and failed attempts. They tend to blame themselves regardless of the actual cause. This would then negatively affect their self-confidence and self-esteem.

Explain to your child that failures should be viewed as opportunities to learn and grow. They are also neither absolute nor permanent. Though confidence builds up through repeated successes, failures could help in developing resilience among children. Guide your highly sensitive child into adapting this kind of mentality so that their self-confidence would not take a massive hit whenever they make mistakes or fail at achieving their goals.

5. Teach your child effective visualization techniques.

Studies show that visualization is an effective way of turning one's thoughts into reality. Simply speaking, it helps you prepare your body and mind into actually doing what must be done to attain the outcome you want.

Highly sensitive children are known for the capacity to think things deeply. As such, visualization tends to be a compatible approach for them to gain more confidence.

How does this work?

One good way to apply this technique is by teaching your child to visualize the good things that could happen in the future. For example, if your child is going to perform a song at the upcoming school assembly, help them imagine what it would be like if they performed well— the sound of applause from the audience, the smiles on the faces of their teachers, classmates, and other students, as well as the praise that they may receive from others.

Letting your child focus on the positive side of

things would make them more willing and more confident about doing something while also keeping his/her mind away from the stressful or worrying parts.

6. Allow your child to try to solve problems without your help.

   Avoid interfering immediately. Let your child work through the problem by himself/herself first. If they could figure out a good solution on their own, then their self-confidence would improve.

   Highly sensitive kids tend to take their time in reflecting on their experiences and the challenges they are facing. Observe from afar and give them ample time before offering your help and support.

7. Dissuade your child from engaging in self-criticism.

   Highly sensitive children are known for making mistakes and failures seriously. They bear the burden and consequences of the wrong decisions they make, regardless of whether or not they are truly accountable for them. Moreover, they tend to criticize their character rather than just the behavior or mental process that led them to failure.

Such tendencies are detrimental to building self-confidence. Rather than self-criticism, teach your child how to do self-evaluation instead.

What's the difference between the two?

When you self-criticize, you only focus on what went wrong, and negative labels, such as lazy or incompetent, are applied to one's self. On the other hand, self-evaluation is more constructive. Though it also involves pointing out your shortcomings, self-evaluation requires a reflection about how to improve and how to prevent the recurrence of the mistake. This is important for building confidence because rebounding from failures can only be done if your child can achieve success in their next attempts at the same goals or tasks.

No matter how shy or anxious your highly sensitive child is, everyone is capable of becoming a self-confident individual. With the right guidance and unconditional support from their parents, these kids would be able to feel more confident at communicating with others, building strong relationships, going out of their comfort zones, and achieving their goals in life.

Chapter 14:
Sports and Activities for a Highly Sensitive Child

Due to some characteristics associated with high sensitivity, not every sport or activity would be interesting and enjoyable for HSCs. For example, highly sensitive kids are not fond of performing while under pressure. This pressure may come from their expectations of themselves, from their coach and teammates, or from the thought of having to do well while others are watching.

Many HSCs also do not like high-contact sports and activities that often involve rough and aggressive moves. Competitive sports like football, basketball, or ice hockey are not the usual activities that highly sensitive children would like to engage in.

Noise can also be a determining factor in whether or not an HSC would participate. A sport or activity involving many buzzers, shouting, or loud smacks could be too stimulating for those with high sensitivity. Doing a group performance in front of a large crowd would also be too much to handle for many HSCs.

Still, there are certain types of sports and activities that your highly sensitive child might want to try. In this chapter, we will go over the factors that affect your child's attitude, as well as the recommended sports and activities for those with high sensitivity.

Factors to Consider

Experts suggest that the following factors must be considered when picking a sport or activity that a highly sensitive child could do:

- Age

    Older children have a better idea of what kind of sports and activities they want to do. As such, you may ask for their opinion about a particular activity, and they would be in a better position to decide if they want to push through with your suggestion or not.

    On the other hand, younger HSCs tend to be more resistant when it comes to trying out new sports or activities. Regardless of whether or not it is suitable to your personality and interests, younger ones are less likely to recognize and understand that this change in their daily routine could be good for them. Some parents also note that when they reintroduce the same sports when their children become older, those kids have become much more receptive—some of which ended up adapting the sport or activity as one of their favorite things to do.

- Peers and Environment

  For HSCs, the better way to start a new sport or activity is to join with someone with whom they are already comfortable. For example, some parents register their HSC along with a sibling or a close friend who is also interested in the same sport or activity. The child would feel more at ease to have someone familiar nearby as they try to figure out if what they are doing would be fun for them.

  It would also be helpful if your child could start with a smaller group at first. Eventually, as they become more accepting of the sport or activity, you may encourage them to join a bigger team or group that takes things to a different level.

  Take for example a parent who enrolled her son in to dance class. She invited the daughter of her friend to join as well. The dance studio she had chosen is just a small one that was located near their home. After finishing the course, the child feels ready to learn more about other dancing techniques, so she begins searching for bigger studios that teach more advanced dance lessons for her kid.

- Coach or Host

  In sports, coaches play a vital role in determining the dynamics that would exist within the team. If the coach is solely focused on winning and not on teamwork, then a highly sensitive child would likely not enjoy being in a team that would do anything just to win. Such teams also tend to be full of malicious teasing and bickering—behaviors that would be taken deeply by HSCs.

  Hosts of activities that your child would participate in would also affect their willingness and enjoyment. Forceful or needlessly loud hosts who care more about the audience than the participants would be a big turn-off for HSCs.

Recommended Sports and Activities

What sports or activities should your HSC join? The

ideal answer is anything that they enjoy doing while also feeling comfortable and safe. It should be something that would not cause significant or irreparable damage to their wellbeing and self-esteem.

In case that your child is not quite sure about what kinds of sports or activities would fit these criteria, here are some good options to consider:

- Cycling
- Golf
- Running/Sprinting
- Swimming
- Hiking
- Yoga
- Any skills-enhancement class

As you have learned in this chapter, sports and other activities may still be fun and enjoyable for those with high sensitivity. Give your child enough time to warm up to their choice, and assure them that it is okay to quit if they realize that it is not making them feel happy or fulfilled at all.

Since not every HSC would react the same way, feel free to encourage your child to try out other sports that are not listed in this book. You might end up being surprised when your child thrives while doing competitive sports or group performances, too.

Chapter 15:
Anger Management

Do you think your highly sensitive child has a bad temper? Are they prone to bursting out in anger? Are they easily irritated by people or the things around them?

If you answer "yes" to any of these questions, then your child needs to learn how to better manage their feelings of anger. More often than not, this anger stems from overstimulation. In such cases, they get annoyed or frustrated by what they are sensing from their environment. HSCs also have intense emotions, so something that would have been trivial only to others with less sensitivity could be a big issue for them.

Parents should teach their highly sensitive kids the proper and healthy way to handle their anger, as well as how to minimize the effect of their anger triggers on them. The following sections will cover how you should go about this.

Identifying Anger-Related Behavior Patterns

An anger management plan should be based on the root cause of your child's anger episodes. Otherwise, your strategies would likely be ineffective and may even cause more harm than good.

If you cannot think of the probable root cause, consider observing and writing down your child's behavioral patterns. Take the time to record the contributing factors to their temper or outburst and their level of anger as well. Do this for at least a week to get a more comprehensive understanding of your child's anger management issues.

Here are some guide questions that you could refer to make more systematic and objective observations:

a. Family
   o   Does your child's temper flare up when they are interacting with you or their siblings?
   o   Does your child get upset when they have to do chores at home?
b. School
   o   Does your child show signs of anger right before going to school?
   o   Is the child struggling with his lessons at school?
   o   Have you heard anything from school that your child is being bullied?

       o   Does your child have friends at school?

c. Other Activities

       o   Does your child get angry when he/she fails to win a game?

       o   Does your child become angry when he/she could not learn a new skill?

Go over your observations and highlight the common and recurring themes. See if time or day is a factor that could be triggering their anger episodes, too. Those are the behavioral patterns that you need to focus on to better address your child's need for guidance when it comes to managing their anger.

Recommended Anger Management Strategies

Now that you are aware of the likely causes of your child's anger, you should begin thinking of ways on how you could break the patterns and resolve the underlying issues. Below are 4 strategies that have been observed to effective for those dealing with highly sensitive children:

Strategy No. 1: Learn how to react properly to your child's anger.

Many parents who are shocked by their child's outburst tend to feel angry as well. This could be even more likely if you are also highly sensitive. However, resist as much as you can from reacting badly right away. Otherwise, you would fail to calm down your child well enough to talk about their feelings; you might even make things worse by saying or doing unintentional yet harmful things to your child.

What you can do is practice calming techniques so that you can remain clearheaded even when you are on the receiving end of your child's anger. Yes, this would take some time to become part of your habit, but extending the effort to do so would be beneficial for your relationship with your child and your goal of teaching them better ways to handle their anger.

Strategy No. 2: Refrain from immediately punishing your child for being angry.

Since anger-related behaviors are normally negative, your instinct might be telling you that you need to punish your child for dissuading them from doing such behaviors. It could seem like the right thing that you should do as a parent during that exact moment. However, studies show that doling out a punishment right away would teach your highly sensitive child the wrong lesson—that is, they are not allowed to feel anger for any reason.

This does not mean that you should just let your kid get away with their bad behaviors whenever they feel angry. Rather than punish them though, you should calm them down or wait until they feel calm enough to listen to your guidance and lessons about the proper and healthy way to express their anger.

Strategy No. 3: Allow your child to have enough time to cool down.

As explained in the previous strategy, highly sensitive children need time to process their feelings and calm down their emotions. Forcing them to talk to you while they are still angry would probably cause more resentment and misunderstanding between the two of you.

While you may hasten the process by leaving them be in a spot where they could remain undisturbed, it is best to avoid intervening too much as they reflect on what they are feeling at that moment. Remember to reassure your child that you are there for them once they are ready to talk about what happened. Until then, keep watch over them from a distance, and look out for signs that it might escalate into a meltdown.

Strategy No. 4: Empathize with your child.

Doing this will make your child feel validated about their anger. Yes, acting out in anger is bad, but feeling angry is not necessarily so. It is a normal emotion that anyone could feel, and your child has to understand the difference between the two. They will be more open to listening to what you have to say about this matter if you would refrain from criticizing or downplaying their feelings.

To show that you empathize with them, first, you must listen to their thoughts and explanation about their anger. Then, tell them that you understand why they have become angry or that you would likely feel the same way if you were in their shoes. Once you have gotten your child's full attention, start pointing out the wrong things they did while angry, such as yelling, destroying things, hurting themselves or others, and explaining why such behaviors are wrong. Remember to teach them how to do better the next time they feel like acting that way again.

In case that your child's anger is based on a recurring issue, make an effort to intervene, and you're your child in resolving that issue. After all, the last strategy would not work out so well if the child starts becoming helpless about their situation. They might not even listen to what you have to say next time since you only taught them how to react but not how to effectively address what is causing their anger in the first place. Learning how to manage anger is important, but it is equally important to reduce your child's likelihood of feeling angry because of things that are within control.

Chapter 16:
Telling the Difference Between Tantrums and Sensory Meltdowns

M any people believe tantrums and meltdowns are synonymous with one another. From an outsider's perspective, both appear the same, especially among kids. However, as you will learn in this chapter, the two are different in terms of their causes, signs, and resolutions.

Let's go over each for you to better understand the proper way to handle them in case your highly sensitive child goes through them.

What is a Tantrum?

Tantrums happen as a result of either anger or frustration. In general, behaviors associated with this include yelling, crying, and holding the breath in. More often than not, the child still has some degree of control over their actions while throwing a tantrum, which means that they have the ability and capacity to stop this on their own.

According to experts, tantrums are triggered by the

following:

- Desire to get something
- Urge to avoid something
- Frustration over something
- Failure to communicate what they need or want

Given this, a tantrum will stop once the child has gotten what they want, avoided the thing they do not want to do or experience, or when they have given up. Take note, however, that in some instances, tantrums may escalate into a meltdown, depending on the circumstances and the child's predisposition.

To better help you recognize the signs of a tantrum, check if your child is aware of their surroundings and the people nearby. A child who is throwing a tantrum tends to pay attention to what is happening around them so that they can change their behaviors accordingly. In most situations, they will try to match the reactions of the people who have noticed them.

This means that if they think you are starting to give in, the child may either amp up their tantrum or start to wind down since they believe that they will get what they want soon. On the other hand, if they see little to no reaction from you, they would soon realize that this tactic is not working out that well for them so they are likely going to stop throwing a tantrum.

What is a Sensory Meltdown?

A sensory meltdown occurs when the child is feeling incredibly overwhelmed. Because of too much stimulation, a child with a meltdown tends to yell or cry—reactions that bear similarities with someone with a tantrum. However, what differentiates a meltdown is that the child would often either "shut down" themselves or run away from the environment or people who are causing their meltdown. Moreover, meltdowns are beyond the child's control because it is not just an emotional reaction but rather a full-bodied one that is so intense and numbing at the same time.

Meltdowns happen for a variety of reasons, such as:

- Too many stimuli to process at the same time
- Extreme frustration
- Unexpected and sudden changes

Sometimes, parents are not aware of what is triggering the meltdown. As a result, they become confused or helpless about how to react properly. To keep this from happening to you, keep in mind these other signs of a sensory meltdown:

141

- Your child loses the ability to control their actions, communicate, or resolve the situation on their own.

- Your child fails to notice what is going on around them.

- Your child does not react to what others are saying or doing.

- Your child starts to either panic, withdraw to themselves, or run away from you or other people.

You may be able to help a child who is experiencing a meltdown by changing their environment or stop whatever was happening before the meltdown. However, if you cannot do so, meltdowns may stop on their own once the child has worn themselves out. This is not an ideal outcome because a meltdown is going to take a toll on your child—physically, mentally, and emotionally.

Suggested Strategies on Handling Tantrums and Sensory Meltdowns

Given that the true nature of tantrums and sensory meltdowns are different, the way to manage and defuse them are also different. As explained earlier, tantrums are intentional, and the child has an end goal in sight, while meltdowns are pure and uncontrollable reactions towards stimuli. This means that you can handle tantrums by addressing what the child wants or needs. On the other hand, it is much harder to help a child experiencing a meltdown because not even the child knows what they need or want at that moment.

Still, experts have devised ways on how parents could properly stop a tantrum and a sensory meltdown. Let's go over these recommendations so that you would be better equipped to handle such instances in the future:

A. Tantrums

Simply giving in to your child's demands is not the answer unless it is essential for their health, safety, or general welfare. For example, if your child throws a tantrum over a toy that he wants you to buy for him, then purchasing that toy just to make him stop would teach him the wrong lesson.

To deal with tantrums without giving in to your child, you must first acknowledge the cause of the tantrum. Tell your child that you are aware of why he is behaving this way and that you are willing to listen to what he has to say if he would refrain from yelling, crying, or whatever tantrum-related behavior he is doing.

Once he has calmed down enough to listen more to you, explain to your child a better and more appropriate way of letting you know of his needs or wants. After all, he might be throwing a tantrum just because he does not understand any other way to get your attention or to make you agree with their request.

Since praises and rewards help reinforce good behaviors, remember to acknowledge your child's effort in listening to your teachings when he does not have a tantrum the next time he needs or wants something. Whether you would go through with his request is in your discretion, but in terms of dissuading your child from throwing a tantrum, praising him for his appropriate behavior and then explaining why he will or will not get what he needed or wanted could be a good response for you to give.

B. Sensory Meltdowns

A child's meltdown can end either through fatigue or by lessening the sensory information they receive. The latter is the healthier and faster way to handle this, especially since there is no guarantee that the child would wear themselves out quickly.

Given this, it would be best if you could find a quiet, comfortable, and safe place for your child. For instance, if your child suddenly suffers a meltdown while he is accompanying you to the supermarket, you could help your child get out of it by leaving the supermarket and heading back to your car. Stay there with them without trying to talk to them in an attempt to calm them down. What your child needs is time, not reassuring words or touches. More often than not, children find the mere presence of their parents to be soothing already.

Understanding the difference between tantrums and sensory meltdowns is a critical factor in helping your highly sensitive child to get through either of them. Pay attention to what usually triggers these behaviors and reactions from your child so that you would know what situations to avoid and so that you could be better prepared to handle them in the future.

Chapter 17:
Tips to End the Bedtime Battles and Getting Your HSC to Sleep

According to Dr. Aron, highly sensitive children need more sleep than children without this trait. They would benefit from longer sleep because this downtime enables them to recover from a day's worth of processing more stimuli than an average person does. As such, she recommends to parents to pay more attention not just to the length of sleep but also to the quality of sleep that highly sensitive children get.

There are several ways on how to help your child get the right number of high-quality sleep. Below are 8 tips that are simple yet effective at achieving these goals:

Tip No. 1: Get the timing right.

Allocate enough time for your child's bedtime routine. Experts suggest adjusting to an earlier schedule since highly sensitive children need more time to wind down and relax. As such, many parents opt to start the bedtime routine at least 45 minutes before their children have to sleep.

The exact timing for this routine depends on how early your child has to wake up the following morning. Since the time is not fixed, count back from their wake-up time until you reach the ideal number of sleeping hours for kids. Depending on your child's age, this can range from 8 to 12 hours per day.

Tip No. 2: Consider what your child wants to do as part of their bedtime routine.

More often than not, children do not like the idea of having to go to bed earlier than they want to. As a result, they would likely resist your attempts to start their bedtime routine early too.

What you can do to get their cooperation is to explain and show them that the routine does not mean that they have to go to bed immediately. Instead, this should be seen as a time to bond together. It would convince them even more if you could incorporate activities that they consider fun or relaxing into their bedtime routine, such as reading a book, listening to lullabies, or simply just talking with you about their day.

Tip No. 3: Stick to the sleeping schedule.

Since highly sensitive children take more time to adjust to changes in their daily routine, the key to speeding up the process and making sure that it would turn into a habit is consistency. Let the bedtime routine be a normal and predictable part of your child's day-to-day activities.

Yes, there might be times when your child would not meet the schedule, but try to keep such occasions to a minimum. Over time, you would notice that your child will require little to no prompt to begin the bedtime routine, thus lessening the stress and effort that it could cause to both you and your child.

Tip No. 4: Remove distractions.

You can begin this by roping in your child in putting away their toys and other things to their proper places. Then, turn off the electronic screens, such as mobile phones, tablets, and television, in their sleeping area. Studies show that the blue light from such devices could prevent children from falling asleep.

Tip No. 5: Create a soothing atmosphere.

Dim the lights or just turn on the bedside lamp that gives off softer lighting. Highly sensitive children tend to respond well to soothing music or relaxing sounds. Make sure that the temperature in your child's sleeping area is neither too hot nor too cold as well.

Tip No. 6: Read a book to your child.

As explained earlier, certain activities may be incorporated into the bedtime routine of highly sensitive children. Among these, reading a book together seems to be one of the most preferred activities of both children and parents. Why?

Reading a book together is not just a learning opportunity but also a time to strengthen the bond as well. Depending on the book, this activity may help increase the child's vocabulary, teach them valuable life lessons and morals, and improve the communication between parents and their children.

If reading is not a preferred activity for your child, consider singing a bedtime song together instead. It could be a great way to enhance your child's talents and skills while also creating good memories between you and your child.

Tip No. 7: Talk about the day your child had.

Highly sensitive children have many thoughts and emotions that they need to get out of their system before calming down. As such, it would be helpful for them if you could set aside time to listen to them talk about their experiences, ideas, and even worries and fears before they go to bed.

In the latter case, please make an effort to alleviate these negative thoughts and reassure them that the next day would be better. This would help calm down their emotions and put away their anxieties and doubts, even if it is just for the night.

As a parent, remember to pay attention to these negative thoughts and see if your intervention is already needed. Though it would be in your child's best interest for them to forget these concerns, significant issues must be addressed immediately to prevent them from causing more harm to your child in the future.

Tip No. 8: Try guided meditation for kids.

Nowadays, recordings of guided meditation or other mindfulness activities that are specifically developed for children may be easily purchased or downloaded. These could be of great help for nights when your child needs extra help calming down their thoughts and emotions.

It might take some time for them to learn how to this properly. Still, with your support and regular practice, meditation and mindfulness practices could be beneficial not just for the bedtime routine of highly sensitive children but also to keep them from feeling overwhelmed during the day.

Consider doing these strategies to improve the quality and lengthen the sleep of your child. Remember to listen to your child's opinions, too. Do not make their bedtime routine a chore or a demand so that you will get their cooperation and commitment to stick to the routine.

Chapter 18:

Help Your HSC Go from Fearful to Having Fun at Celebrations and Special Events

Usually, children find celebrations and special events as fun and exciting. They get to play with other kids, be free from chores or assignments, eat good food, and be doted upon by the adults. However, due to their high sensitivity, HSCs tend to feel stressed, anxious, and overwhelmed during such events, especially when they become too stimulated. Because of this, they do not enjoy attending celebrations, often to the point of wanting to completely avoid them.

As parents, you can help your highly sensitive child be more open-minded about taking part in fun, social gatherings, and guiding them into having fun by themselves, with you, or with the other attendees. Check out the tips given below to find out how you can make this happen for your HSC:

Tip No. 1: Talk in advance with the hosts and other attendees, if possible, about the needs and preferences of your child.

Share with the hosts and other attendees about what they should expect in terms of how your child would likely behave during the event. Doing so would prevent others from forcing your child into participating in activities that they do not enjoy, such as games and spontaneous performances.

Give them a heads up about sensitive topics that should be avoided, too. For example, if your child does not feel comfortable talking about their school life due to bullying or problems in their academic performance, then ask others to refrain from asking questions related to school. Your goal is to ensure that your child would not fear socializing with others, so it is best if you could keep them in their comfort zone, especially since they would already have to deal with being bombarded by different types of stimuli during the celebration.

Tip No. 2: Plan activities for your child ahead of time.

Think of activities that your child could occupy, especially if they tend to feel antsy when they are in the company of unfamiliar people. Consider bringing their favorite books or toys that they could either play with on their own or share with other kids they are close with. Come with a variety of activities for your child so that they would have options on what to do in case they do not want to socialize and join the festivities.

Tip No. 3: Check if your child could have downtime when they need it.

Noise, crowd, bright lights, humid temperature—there plenty of environmental factors that could overstimulate your highly sensitive child. In case that your child starts becoming overwhelmed during the event, you should be able to guide them into a quiet, secluded space and with minimal sources of visual stimulation such as flashy colors or clutter.

To do so, scope out the venue of the event and

find areas that could be a suitable spot for your child to calm down if they need to. Talk this over with the event host so that they know what you are planning to use the space for during the event.

Tip No. 4: Check the menu.

Many highly sensitive children tend to have sensory aversions to certain types of food. To keep them from starving during the event, make sure to check out the items in the menu that the host is planning to serve to their guests. Go over each to see if there is something that does not agree with your child's food preferences.

Since you cannot simply request for a menu change just because your child does not like eating something, pack and bring food that your child likes to the celebration. Again, it would be polite to let your host know ahead of time to avoid offending or worrying them about the menu for the event.

Though some parents think that event menus are good opportunities for their kids to try out something new, highly sensitive children would appreciate it more if they would gradually familiarize themselves with these new food items before eating them.

Tip No. 5: Discuss with your child what they should expect during the event.

Once you are better informed about the specifics of the event, as well as your plans for your child, take the time to sit down with them and share the details. Let them know who would be attending the event so that they would not be surprised in case there would be unfamiliar people around them during the celebration.

Tell your child as well that they could approach you if they feel like doing something else or if they need some peace amid the event. This would make them feel more assured that they could have fun at their own pace, even while outside the comforts of your home.

Don't forget to share the menu for the event with them, as well as the things you have packed for them. Listen to what they have to say about these so that you would have time to prepare their other requests if there are any.

Helping your child get over their worries and doubts about social events would not just allow them to gain new experiences but also show them how they could have fun at such gatherings. In the long term, these efforts are going to pay off when your highly sensitive child grows up to become a happy and well-adjusted adult.

Part 3:

Highly Sensitive Children and School

Chapter 19:
Choosing the Perfect School for Your Highly Sensitive Child

Finding the ideal school for highly sensitive children can be tough, especially since the standards of non-progressive ones tend to be unsuitable for these kids. While this is understandable since many schools face challenges when it comes to facilities, qualified teachers, and training, you do not have to just settle for whatever school is near your house.

To ensure that your child would grow up to become a healthy and well-adjusted individual, you should pay more attention to getting them into the right school. In this chapter, we will go over the qualities of a good school for your HSC.

The Ideal Teachers for Highly Sensitive Children

Not all kinds of teaching styles would be compatible with the needs of a highly sensitive student. Since teachers are critical factors in the success of your child at school, you need to carefully evaluate if the teachers from the schools that you are considering would meet the criteria set out below:

- Acknowledge High Sensitivity as a Trait

  Teachers should also believe and understand that high sensitivity is a normal trait to have—not a mental disorder that needs to be treated. With this, you can be assured that someone at school would reassure your child that being sensitive is okay, especially if their peers do not understand this yet.

  It would be great if the teachers also know how to recognize a highly sensitive child, as well as the signs of children who are feeling overwhelmed or those who are experiencing a sensory meltdown.

- Gentle and Caring Attitude

  The teachers should be constructive yet firm when it comes to dealing with poor performances or bad behaviors. You do not want someone who raises their voice at children or makes groundless accusations. Instead, look for genuinely caring teachers who view each student as an individual who has different interests, personalities and may need to get things done in a specific way.

- Knowledge in Mindfulness

Nowadays, special courses for teachers are available to train them about the various techniques that could be applied to encourage mindfulness among their students. Check if the teachers from that school are equipped with this kind of training, and better yet, if the school includes mindfulness activities as part of the curriculum.

The Perfect School Environment for Highly Sensitive Children

In terms of the overall school environment, the perfect one for your child is quiet yet cozy—something that would remind them of home. It should preferably have greeneries and raises pets that students could interact with. Bright lights or too much visual clutter are also not good for highly sensitive kids since they may cause overstimulation.

Child development experts have long advocated for smaller class sizes, wherein there would only be about 18 to 22 students per classroom. Since not every country has regulations that have considered this, you should make it a point to check the standard class size and average classroom area of the schools you are evaluating for your child. After all, studies show that these would significantly affect how highly sensitive a child would feel and perform while in class.

Besides class and classroom size, the seating arrangement also matters in how well your child would flourish at school. Ideally, they should not be seated near noisy children or those who have been observed to be unruly. Check if the school accommodates seating requests like these, and ask if they would give you advance notice in case that seating arrangements would be changed.

The school must also have provisions for your child to have some downtime when they need it. Again, many schools are not equipped with such mainly due to space restrictions. However, it would be great if you could find one that has at least one of the following:

- Accessible, safe, and comfortable quiet spots that are not visually stimulating
- Sound-proofing in all or several classrooms
- Noise-canceling headphones for children
- Reading corners where loud or boisterous activities are not allowed.

Recommended School Activities for Highly Sensitive Children

Certain school activities can help teach highly sensitive kids how to enhance their strengths and manage their shortcomings. For example, lessons and plays that center around self-compassion may help them overcome their tendency to blame themselves whenever something goes wrong.

In terms of school hours, some HSC finds the regular school hours to be quite draining. If this is the case for your child as well, their school needs to either have shorter school hours or be more flexible when it comes to allowing half-days in case your child needs it. Look into the possibility of a combined school and home-schooling approach to lessen the time your child would spend at school.

These children also tend to thrive better when there is enough downtime in between classes, wherein they can fully process their thoughts and recover from the stimulation they received from the previous class. Lunch breaks and recess time could be hard experiences for many HSC because of overstimulation. It would be great if the school provides options for students who do not want to spend their breaks on the playground or cafeteria—for example, a quiet resting area where the students could read quietly, draw, or just simply rest on their own.

Since highly sensitive children need more time to accept changes in their routine or expectations, advance notice about any changes to the class or school activity schedule should also be given by the school. Through this, you would also have enough time to help your child adjust and transition to the new schedule.

To further help you evaluate the potential schools for your children, use this set of questions as a guide in your assessment:

1. On average, how many students are there in a class?
2. What is the ratio between the teachers and the students?
3. Are there any specialists or trained personnel in the school who understand the needs of a highly sensitive child?
4. How does the school support the development of children in terms of academic performance, social difficulties, and emotional challenges?
5. How does the school handle a case that requires disciplinary action?

6. How do the school environment and class-rooms look like?

7. What time do the classes start and end?

8. What kind of student activities does the school have?

9. How many and how long are the breaks during the entire school day?

10. How does the school communicate with the parents and/or guardians of the students?

Refer to this questionnaire while evaluating each school, and remember to record your responses in written form so that you can better compare and make a decision later on. It is best to go over your top options with your child as well so that you can get their opinion about which school they want to go to. After all, it is your child who would be spending hours at school without you all the time to guide and support them.

Chapter 20:

Tips for Teachers Working with Highly Sensitive Students

Some parents assume that it is improper to disclose to teachers about the high sensitivity of their children, fearing that doing so might make them seem like they are overstepping the line. However, child development experts argue that teachers have to know these aspects of their students' personalities to better foster and guide them at school.

Below are ten valuable tips that you could share with the teachers responsible for your child's education. Feel free to share these tips with them and other parents so that your child would have a more pleasant and fruitful time as a student:

Tip No. 1: Communicate with parents about the needs and preferences of their highly sensitive child.

Teachers are not mindreaders. Take the time to discuss with parents the sensitivities of your students. Since these tend to manifest differently from when the child is at home, inquire about the child's past experiences when they were at school or when they are in public spaces. Having this knowledge would help you to better prepare to meet the needs and observe the preferences of your highly sensitive students, which would then enable them to focus more on performing well at school.

Tip No. 2: Pay attention to seating arrangements.

Highly sensitive children get easily distracted by the various things that their seatmates would do during the class. If it becomes too much for them to handle, this could eventually cause them to become irritable, sometimes to the point of overstimulation.

They can also be affected if they are seated near the classroom door, near the window where they could hear the buzzing of people and activities outside, or near noisy classroom equipment such as a loud electric fan or an electric pencil sharpener. Being seated under bright overhead lights could also cause overstimulation in some cases.

Tip No. 3: Test scores do not fully reflect the abilities and aptitude of highly sensitive children.

Studies show that highly sensitive children do not do as well as others when undergoing traditional testing means. More often than not, they become too overwhelmed by the time pressure of formal exams. They take more time than usual in coming up with answers, which sometimes leads to overthinking and doubting themselves.

Teachers should consider these characteristics brought about by high sensitivity and modify the mechanics of an examination as needed to better assess their students' academic performance. It would also help if teachers would further support their students by doing calming activities before administering the test itself.

Tip No. 4: Generalized scolding or punishments have a greater impact on highly sensitive children.

Making a sweeping accusation or reprimand to

the class could be devastating for HSCs. They take matters personally and deeply, regardless if they are truly at fault or not. Other children might be as affected as they are, so the effect of the scolding or punishment would be felt more by those with high sensitivity. That is why teachers should opt to dole out disciplinary actions away from students involved in the matter unless the situation calls for a general scolding or punishment.

When reprimanding a highly sensitive person, teachers should adopt a gentle approach. Pay special attention to the tone and volume of the voice, as well as facial expressions, since HSCs are keen observers. Harsh criticisms and violent reactions tend to have a dire impact on these children, and rather than be corrective, the reprimand becomes a deterrent for the student to try and do better next time.

Tip No. 5: Give highly sensitive children enough time to adjust to new situations or people.

Highly sensitive children are known for being slow to warm up to new or unfamiliar surroundings and people. This applies in whatever location or scenario they are in, including at school. These kids prefer to observe first quietly and from a distance until they have a better read of the situation, the environment, or the person.

Rather than immediately labeling the student as shy, cold, or disinterested, teachers should allow HSCs enough time to process new information and get used to the changes and new stimuli around them—whether it is meeting new teachers, getting to know new classmates, or doing new school activities.

Tip No. 6: Allow HSCs to recover for at least 20 minutes when they experience overstimulation.

Due to the large number of stimuli that students receive while at school, there is a chance that you will have to help a highly sensitive child to get through overstimulation. Given this, you should learn first how to recognize the signs of overstimulation and how to handle them properly. If you did spot a student undergoing this, lead them into a quiet spot where they could calm down.

Studies show that HSCs need at least 20 minutes to go back to their functional and responsive states. Since that amount of time is relatively long, it would be better if you could learn how to prevent its occurrence. Experts recommend adding a predetermined quiet time for the students so that they could decompress and regain their energy for the next classes or activities they would do at school.

Tip No. 7: Harness the inherent creativity of HSCs.

Students with high sensitivity tend to be more attuned with their creative side—whether it is writing stories, making art, or performing a musical piece. They also get inspired by scenes of nature, especially when it makes them feel at peace. Encourage these students to go after their creative pursuits by incorporating activities that would allow this aspect of their personality to shine through.

Tip No. 8: Break large tasks into manageable chunks.

Big activities, projects, assignments, or performances at school could be quite overwhelming for highly sensitive students. Rather than force them to absorb and do everything right away, break down their tasks into smaller and doable steps that ultimately lead to the fulfillment of the big task you have in mind. Make sure to set specific goals for each so they would get a sense of accomplishment as they work their way through each step.

Tip No. 9: Give HSC positive feedback when it is due.

Just as HSC takes criticisms deeply, these students are also greatly affected by praise and recognition from teachers and their peers. Remember to give them positive feedback whenever they do something well, which may be done in various ways such as highlighting the exceptional points they have done, giving them a high score as they deserve, or stamping their works with your seal of approval.

Tip No. 10: Pay attention to your condition.

> As explained earlier, HSCs have heightened senses and perception. They would notice changes in your appearance and behavior, especially since they would see you regularly at school. If they believe that you are stressed out, unwell, or in pain, these observations would cause distress to your highly sensitive students. Therefore, try to be in your best condition whenever you interact with HSC at school.

The more teachers understand the complexities and nuances of highly sensitive children, the more likely these children would grow and realize their full potential. To achieve this, communication and cooperation between them and you as the parent should be established and maintained throughout your child's schooling years.

Chapter 21:
Questions to Ask Your Highly Sensitive Child After School

If your highly sensitive child only gives succinct or vague answers whenever you inquire about their day at school, then you are likely asking the wrong questions. HSCs may hesitate to share their thoughts and experiences for a variety of reasons. Regardless of the cause, however, you could get them to open up to you and talk about the good and bad experiences they have while in school.

To help you accomplish this feat, here are suggested points of inquiry that you should consider asking your highly sensitive child:

Questions Related to School Lessons and Activities

- o What books have you read during your break time?
- o What games did you play at school today?

Questions Related to Personal Experiences

- o What is your favorite class or lesson for today?
- o What was the best thing that you did earlier?
- o What was the worst thing that happened to you at school earlier?
- o Did you find any school rules hard to follow earlier?
- o Did any of today's school lessons or activities frustrated you?

Questions Related to Personal Feelings

- o Did something make you smile or laugh today while at school?
- o Did you feel worried during your lessons/break?
- o Did you feel full/happy after eating your lunch and snacks?
- o What are you feeling most proud of today?

Questions Related to Other People

- o If you could pick your seatmate for a day, who would it be?

o Was there anyone absent from your class today?

o Did someone help you out with something earlier?

o What is the best thing you like about your teacher?

o What is something that you wish your teacher would not do?

o Who did you eat your lunch or snack with?

o Who did you play with today?

o Did anyone get hurt in the playground earlier?

o Was there anyone who seemed mean to you or others?

Questions Related to Future School Experiences

o What are you looking forward to when you go to school tomorrow?

o Are there any school activities that you are feeling excited about?

You do not have to ask all of these questions each day. Mix things up to better understand the different aspects of your child's school life. It would also keep your school-related conversations interesting for both you and your child.

Timing is also essential when it comes to asking questions. Avoid firing away just after they have gotten home from school. Let them rest and have a snack first to recover from the day they had. Some parents opt to ask these questions over dinner so that other family members could also inquire about the experiences of the HSC while at school.

Others believe that some questions are better suited to be asked during the bedtime routine. After all, many kids would likely grab the opportunity to delay their sleeping time. Stick to light and positive questions though to avoid riling up your child before they go to sleep.

When your child responds to your question, remember to pay attention to their non-verbal cues, such as facial expressions, tone of voice, posture, and hand gestures. Look for patterns in their behavior so that you could gain more insight into what they are saying in between the lines. Through this, you may be able to further help your child to have a better experience while they are at school.

Chapter 22:
Sensitive Boys Can Be the Perfect Target for Bullies

According to studies, the distribution of the high sensitivity trait is equal between males and females. Given that 1 in 5 people possesses this trait, it also means that 1 in 5 boys are highly sensitive.

Due to cultural norms and social expectations, boys who exhibit the qualities associated with high sensitivity become prime targets for bullying. Most bullying-related incidents occur at school, which causes highly sensitive boys to suffer from poor academic performance, depression, and in extreme cases, they could even commit suicide.

Bullies tend to target those who are different from them. They also prefer those who do not fight back and those who show a reaction to their bullying. Therefore, the unique aspects of HSC's personality as well as their avoidant approach to violence and overactive emotions attract the attention of bullies.

As a parent, you could protect your highly sensitive son from bullying by guiding them into strengthening their character and abilities, as well as helping them bolster their social support while at school. To learn more about how you could achieve these goals, let's go over the five strategies to keep your highly sensitive child from bullying.

Strategy No. 1: Help your son build his self-confidence.

Child development experts have explained that children become more confident in facing challenges in the outside world if they receive unconditional love and support at home. The responsibility does not just fall under yours though. Children benefit from strong and loving relationships with other adult members of the extended family, such as their grandparents, uncles, and aunts.

More often than not, mothers spend more time nurturing and teaching their kids. However, to help your son be more self-confident, they also need to have a good relationship with the male members of the family.

Why?

Highly sensitive boys look up to them as role

models. The way the male adults in the family behave and treat them profoundly influences the development of these boys. Though fathers could teach their sons how to stand up for themselves in the face of bullies, they should also accept that the true nature of their children's personalities. Acknowledging and understanding that their son is highly sensitive would keep them from attempting to change their children's characters. In the long run, showing this kind of acceptance and support would your son be more self-confident even when challenged by other kids at school.

Strategy No. 2: Boost your son's self-esteem.

Highly sensitive boys who feel dissatisfaction about certain parts of their selves are more negatively affected by bullying. As a result, their self-esteem takes more hits if others point out the parts that they do not like about themselves.

Parents could counteract these effects by highlighting the best parts instead and then guiding their sons into focusing more on those aspects of their being. Highly sensitive boys tend to be more in touch with their inner selves too, so encourage them into practicing mindfulness activities, such as meditation and saying positive affirmations to themselves.

Thriving in a world that is less than accepting of their high sensitivity would be much easier for boys if they feel comfortable in their skin. Appreciating the fact that they are different would make them feel stronger and more confident even when facing their bullies.

Strategy No. 3: Guide your son into becoming more physically fit.

As much as 85% of highly sensitive boys do not participate in team sports according to research. Given their preference for being alone, it should not come as a surprise that most of them enjoy doing physical activities on their own.

Their dislike of team sports stems from their avoidant tendencies. They do not perform well under pressure, especially when other members of the group cause it. These boys are also easily affected by harsh words and teasing, which usually occurs among boys who mock and bully others while playing.

Whether or not your son has good athletic abilities, you should still encourage them into doing physical activities, including team sports. Having various experiences would help them grow and develop different aspects of their personality and abilities, thus equipping them with the necessary life skills they need to be successful adults.

Make sure that the sports that your son would engage in are something that interests them. Otherwise, it would likely be a hellish experience that you have forced upon them.

What you can do to protect your child from being bullied while playing team sports is discussing the matter with the coach, trainers, and parents of the other team members. You could also teach your son some effective self-defense techniques that could make them feel empowered if they encounter bullies while doing sports.

Strategy No. 4: Encourage your son to form strong friendships.

On average, boys tend to be part of relatively large friendship groups. In comparison, highly sensitive boys prefer socializing with just one friend—though they also enjoy spending time on their own.

While these children should stick to what makes them feel comfortable, it could also be helpful for them to learn how to interact with other boys who are not highly sensitive as well, especially in preventing them from being bullied. Discuss with them the importance of having friends who respect their limits and boundaries. Show them how friendships could take different forms—not just what they usually see at school. Your goal here is to encourage your son to strike a balance between their need to spend time alone and their willingness to spend quality time with friends who may help and support them in case they get bullied at school.

Strategy No. 5: Ensure that your son feels safe while he is at school.

Responsible parents know that protecting their children at school means reaching out not just to the teachers but also to the other parents and volunteering for school activities. This would strengthen your presence in the school as your son's guardian and send out a message that you would not stand for the mistreatment of your child by their peers or even school staff.

In case of the latter, you should immediately discuss the matter with the teacher involved as well as the school principal. Let them know that you do not find their attitude and behavior toward your son acceptable. Explain why it could be harmful to your son's development, and try to make them understand where you are coming from. If neither the teacher nor the school is responsive and willing to change, then it would be in your child's best interest if you would transfer him to a more open-minded and genuinely caring school.

If your son is in danger of physical harm while

they are in school, inform the school immediately so that they could intervene. If they do not respond, then contact the police right away. Physical violence due to bullying incidences could cause irreparable damage to your child and might even escalate to fatal consequences.

As a last note, studies show that many highly sensitive boys thrive more when they are home-schooled. Consider this option for your son so that he can learn and pursue his interests at their own pace and without worrying about school bullies.

Conclusion

I'd like to thank you and congratulate you for transiting my lines from start to finish.

I hope this book was able to help you to discover and learn about the ideal parenting strategies that can help you nurture well your highly sensitive child. Though it is a perfectly normal trait to have, these children would thrive more and become happy, well-adjusted adults if their needs had been fully met, and they had been guided on how to navigate the world without fearing that they would be ostracized or stigmatized by others because of their unique qualities.

Moreover, I hope you have an in-depth understanding of what it truly means to be a highly sensitive person. Strangers might still apply incorrect labels to your child, but at the very least, you and the people who care about them know not to do so. By now, I also wish that you can explain to others why high sensitivity is not a mental or developmental disorder and how your child does not need treatment—just the consideration and kindness of the people around them.

Now that you are aware of the various parenting strategies that work well for highly sensitive children, take the time to discuss the ones you believe would be suitable for your HSC with the other family members. As explained earlier, you should try your best to get the support and cooperation of the other people involved in taking care of your child. If you don't have one yet, consider adding a pet to your family as well.

Let others know the right way to help your child whenever they feel overstimulated or suffer from a sensory meltdown. Reach out to their teachers, the parents of their friends, and even the close friends of your child. You would not always be there for them, but at least you can be assured that someone else would know what to do to keep your child safe.

Encourage your HSC to explore their interests and develop new skills. Make use of the strategies you have learned about building their self-confidence, figuring out the perfect sports or activities for them, and showing them how to have fun during social gatherings. Having various experiences during their childhood would affect the direction and their motivation for their future pursuits.

High sensitivity does not have to be the defining characteristic of your child. Yes, it will serve as one of the focal points of your parenting strategy, but your child does not have to make their life revolve around this one trait out the many others that they have.

Once again, thank you for reading this book. I wish you the best of luck!

How'd You Enjoy Reading Parenting the Highly Sensitive Child?

I want to say thank you for purchasing and reading this book! I hope you enjoyed it and it's provided value to your life.

If you enjoyed reading this book and found some benefit in it, I'd love your support and hope that you could take a moment to post a review on Amazon. I'd love to hear from you, even if you have feedback, as it'll help me in ensuring that I improve this book and others in the future.

I want to let you know that your review is very important to me and will help this book reach and impact more people's lives.

Thanks for your time and support!

Resources Page

A. (2017, May 16). *How to Help a Highly Sensitive Child Sleep*. Happy Sensitive Kids Blog. https://happysensitivekids.com/2017/05/how-to-help-a-highly-sensitive-child-sleep/

A. (2020, November 11). *25 Things Your Highly Sensitive Child's Teacher Needs to Know*. Happy Sensitive Kids Blog. https://happysensitivekids.com/2017/11/25-things-to-share-with-your-highly-sensitive-childs-teacher/

Acevedo, B. (2021, February 11). *What is Sensory Processing Sensitivity? Traits, Insights, and ADHD Links*. ADDitude. https://www.additudemag.com/highly-sensitive-person-sensory-processing-sensitivity-adhd/

Appleford, S. (2020, March 6). *What is Sensory Food Aversion?* Nutrition For Kids. https://www.nutritionforkids.com.au/learn/what-is-sensory-food-aversion

Belsky, G. (2021, March 31). *What to do when kids refuse to put on certain clothing*. Understood. https://www.understood.org/en/learning-thinking-differences/child-learning-disabilities/sensory-processing-issues/child-refuses-certain-clothes

Boitano, M. (2021, January 20). *Sensory Food Aversion, the Truth About Refusing Textures*. Megan Boitano Nutrition.
https://www.meganboitano.com/blog/sensory-food-aversion-refusing-textures

Checklist of traits in highly sensitive children. (n.d.). Focus on the Family.
https://www.focusonthefamily.ca/content/checklist-of-traits-in-highly-sensitive-children

Daniels, N. (2020, September 30). *Are You an Orchid, a Tulip or a Dandelion?* The New York Times.
https://www.nytimes.com/2020/09/30/learning/are-you-an-orchid-a-tulip-or-a-dandelion.html

Eden, K. (2018, December 29). *The Special Connection Between Highly Sensitive Kids and Pets*. Highly Sensitive Refuge.
https://highlysensitiverefuge.com/highly-sensitive-children-pets/

Eden, K. (2019, May 3). *7 Ways to Help a Highly Sensitive Child Develop Confidence*. Highly Sensitive Refuge.
https://highlysensitiverefuge.com/highly-sensitive-child-confidence/

Ehmke, R. (2020, November 12). *The Family Gathering: A Survival Guide*. Child Mind Institute.
https://childmind.org/article/the-family-gathering-a-survival-guide/

Gaspari, M., Gaspari, M., Price, R., Price, R., Allen, W., Sólo, A., Carvalho, A., White, C., Ubbenga, J., Mulligen, A., Rourke, C. V., Karoliussen, H. B., & Renzi, M. N. (n.d.). *Parenting Archives*. Highly Sensitive Refuge. https://highlysensitiverefuge.com/category/relationships/parenting/

Granneman, J. (2018, May 26). *14 advantages of being highly sensitive*. IntrovertDear.Com. https://introvertdear.com/news/highly-sensitive-person-advantages/

Highly Sensitive Person Traits That Create More Stress. (n.d.). Verywell Mind. https://www.verywellmind.com/highly-sensitive-persons-traits-that-create-more-stress-4126393

Holohan, M. (2018, January 25). *Is your child an orchid, dandelion or tulip? New study examines kids' behavior*. TODAY.Com. https://www.today.com/health/your-child-orchid-dandelion-or-tulip-new-study-examines-kids-t121676

How Much Sleep Do Children Need? (2001, January 1). WebMD. https://www.webmd.com/parenting/guide/sleep-children#1

How People With ADHD Can Cope With Hypersensitivity in Situations. (n.d.). Verywell Mind. https://www.verywellmind.com/sensitivities-and-adhd-20473

How to Parent a Sensitive Child Live in a Less Than Sensitive World. (n.d.). Verywell Family. https://www.verywellfamily.com/parenting-a-sensitive-child-8-discipline-strategies-1094942

Hulsmann, E. (2019, April 8). *7 Secret Benefits of Being a Highly Sensitive Person.* Highly Sensitive Refuge. https://highlysensitiverefuge.com/benefits-highly-sensitive-person/

Is Being an HSP a Disorder? (2021, January 8). Highly Sensitive Refuge. https://highlysensitiverefuge.com/is-hsp-a-disor-der/#The_Difference_Between_HSPs_and_Senso ry_Processing_Disorder_Explained

Jagiellowicz, J. (2020, April 29). *HSP and Sensory Processing Disorder.* Highly Sensitive Society. https://www.highlysensitivesociety.com/blog/hspa ndsensoryprocessingdisorder

Kessler, Z., & Saline, S. P. (2021, February 7). *My Hypersensitivity Is Real: Why Highly Sensitive People Have ADHD.* ADDitude. https://www.additudemag.com/hypersensitivity-disorder-with-adhd/

Lionetti, F. (2018, January 22). *Dandelions, tulips and orchids: evidence for the existence of low-sensitive, medium-sensitive and high-sensitive individuals.* Translational Psychiatry. https://www.nature.com/articles/s41398-017-0090-6?error=cookies_not_supported&code=fa4f770a-2c34-4fb7-bace-5bf32f373459

M. (n.d.). *Celebration and Party Strategies for the Highly Sensitive Child.* Sens. https://thehighlysensitivechild.teachable.com/p/highly-sensitive-celebration-strategies

M. (2018, December 27). *How to End Bedtime Battles with Your Sensitive Child.* The Highly Sensitive Child. https://www.thehighlysensitivechild.com/how-to-end-bedtime-battles-with-your-sensitive-child/

M. (2019a, April 2). *Discipline Strategies for the Sensitive Child.* The Highly Sensitive Child. https://www.thehighlysensitivechild.com/discipline-strategies-for-the-sensitive-child/

M. (2019b, October 21). *8 Questions to Ask when Choosing a School for your Sensitive Child.* The Highly Sensitive Child. https://www.thehighlysensitivechild.com/8-questions-to-ask-when-choosing-a-school-for-your-sensitive-child/

M. (2019c, October 21). *35 Questions to Ask your Highly Sensitive Child After School*. The Highly Sensitive Child.
https://www.thehighlysensitivechild.com/35-questions-to-ask-your-highly-sensitive-child-after-school/

M. (2019d, October 21). *Anger and the Highly Sensitive Child*. The Highly Sensitive Child.
https://web.archive.org/web/20201101090528/https://www.thehighlysensitivechild.com/anger-and-the-highly-sensitive-child/

Morin, A. (2019, October 16). *How to Tell a Tantrum From a Meltdown*. Understood - For Learning and Thinking Differences.
https://www.understood.org/en/learning-thinking-differences/child-learning-disabilities/sensory-processing-issues/compare-the-signs-how-to-tell-a-tantrum-from-a-meltdown

Morin, A. (2021a, March 24). *7 Ways to Help Kids Who Are Sensitive to Taste and Smell*. Understood.
https://www.understood.org/en/learning-thinking-differences/child-learning-disabilities/sensory-processing-issues/7-ways-to-help-your-child-cope-with-taste-sensitivity

Morin, A. (2021b, March 30). *How to cope with sensitivity to touch and textures*. Understood.
https://www.understood.org/en/learning-

thinking-differences/child-learning-disabilities/sensory-processing-issues/tactile-sensitivity-how-to-cope

Morin, A. (2021c, April 2). *The difference between tantrums and meltdowns.* Understood. https://www.understood.org/en/learning-thinking-differences/child-learning-disabilities/sensory-processing-issues/the-difference-between-tantrums-and-meltdowns

New "Highly Sensitive Child" test identifies three groups: orchids, dandelions and tulips. (2018, February 1). Research Digest. https://digest.bps.org.uk/2018/01/11/new-test-of-childrens-environmental-sensitivity-identifies-three-groups-orchids-dandelions-and-tulips/

Raja, D. (2015, March 18). *https://search.google.com/structured-data/testing-tool/336867.* MomJunction. https://www.momjunction.com/articles/parenting-tips-to-handle-a-highly-sensitive-child_00336867/

Rourke, C. V. (2019, October 17). *Highly Sensitive People Have a Special Bond With Animals.* Highly Sensitive Refuge. https://highlysensitiverefuge.com/highly-sensitive-people-have-a-special-bond-with-animals/

Sólo, A. (2020a, March 18). *13 Signs You're a Highly Sensitive Extrovert*. Highly Sensitive Refuge. https://highlysensitiverefuge.com/highly-sensitive-extrovert/

Sólo, A. (2020b, June 18). *The Difference Between Introverts, Empaths, and Highly Sensitive People*. IntrovertDear.Com. https://introvertdear.com/news/the-difference-between-introverts-empaths-and-highly-sensitive-people/

Understanding Sensory Processing Disorder. (n.d.). Understanding Sensory Processing Disorder. https://sensoryhealth.org/basic/understanding-sensory-processing-disorder

Wilding, M. L. (2018, August 25). *The Secret Life of a Highly Sensitive Person - Featured Stories*. Medium. https://medium.com/s/story/the-secret-life-of-a-highly-sensitive-person-e5e49ab4918b

Zeff, T. (2018, December 1). *Parents, Here's How to Prevent Your Sensitive Boy From Being Bullied*. Highly Sensitive Refuge. https://highlysensitiverefuge.com/sensitive-boy-prevent-bullying/

Manufactured by Amazon.ca
Acheson, AB